About the Author

Deepak Gupta is a retired senior executive with fifty years global experience; thirty of them with the Procter & Gamble Company. He has lived and worked in India, Japan, China, Hong Kong, Philippines, and Thailand. This unparalleled exposure to different cultures and traditions has given him excellent insights into people psyche. Deepak decided to write SUCCESS IS A CHOICE to help millions of talented individuals who are unable to succeed beyond a certain point because they lack some inexplicable skills. He aspires to demystify these skills and illustrate how to develop them and reach full potential.

Success is a Choice

Deepak Gupta

Success is a Choice

Olympia Publishers
London

www.olympiapublishers.com
OLYMPIA PAPERBACK EDITION

Copyright © Deepak Gupta 2024

The right of Deepak Gupta to be identified as author of
this work has been asserted in accordance with sections 77 and 78 of
the Copyright, Designs and Patents Act 1988.

All Rights Reserved

No reproduction, copy or transmission of this publication
may be made without written permission.
No paragraph of this publication may be reproduced,
copied or transmitted save with the written permission of the publisher,
or in accordance with the provisions
of the Copyright Act 1956 (as amended).

Any person who commits any unauthorised act in relation to
this publication may be liable to criminal
prosecution and civil claims for damage.

A CIP catalogue record for this title is
available from the British Library.

ISBN: 978-1-80439-563-9

This is a work of fiction.
Names, characters, places and incidents originate from the writer's
imagination. Any resemblance to actual persons, living or dead, is
purely coincidental.

First Published in 2024

Olympia Publishers
Tallis House
2 Tallis Street
London
EC4Y 0AB

Printed in Great Britain

Dedication

To My Lovely Family
Neelam
Aanya – Sareena -- Manav
Noura -- Dhruv

Acknowledgements

In my fifty-year career, I have met many brilliant people who could not succeed beyond a point because they did not have certain skills. I dedicate this book to these wonderful people who are always 'highly valued' but not good enough to make it.

I also thank all my 'gurus' – teachers, bosses, peers, subordinates, customers, suppliers, contractors, friends, and my lovely family – who shaped my experiences and taught me everything I know today. This book is the essence of those learnings.

PREFACE

What is SUCCESS? Who defines it? It is rather difficult to answer these simple questions. SUCCESS may mean different things for different people. Most will describe it in materialistic terms of position, power, career, wealth; some describe it differently. Rarely does anyone consider 'happiness' as 'success,' although everyone will vouch that all their actions are in its pursuit.

Can 'happiness' be the core reason for this unquenching thirst for success? Is materialistic success a precursor and prerequisite for happiness? Are 'we' ourselves, the biggest barrier to 'our' success and happiness, though we invariably assign its cause to things external?

Materialistic success manifests itself in organizations across the world and employees strive to climb the corporate hierarchy; some succeed, others stagnate. Several 'excellent' employees are regularly bypassed by their peers or junior employees. Do the astute and intelligent corporate leaders really choose less-brilliant people? Are the companies unable or unwilling to recognize and reward talent? Is the corporate 'performance yardstick' so ambiguous that an employee feels (s)he is ready for promotion, but the bosses think differently? Is it just favoritism, racism, or gender bias? These are all pertinent questions that often confuse and frustrate employees.

Or is there something else?

SUCCESS IS A CHOICE attempts to answer these crucial

questions through a fictional story. Set in a global company, where the main character Dan Webber works as a senior executive, the tale portrays the effects of the stagnant career on his work and personal life. Unable to bear the disappointment and dissatisfaction, he seeks help from a far more successful younger colleague, Ron Falcon. In the ensuing weeks, Ron takes him on a voyage of exploration, discovery and awareness of the skills that create success, and separate winners. As Dan realizes, learns, and practices the new concepts and skills, he transforms not only himself and his work life but also his deteriorating personal relationships.

One of Dan's major learnings is that only his actions are in his control, not their consequence; the result is an outcome of how well he performs his actions, duties, and responsibilities. He realizes that he has been fretting over results, which were never in his control; the subsequent anxiousness, stress, and frustration compromised what was in his control, his designated actions, unconsciously proving the adage 'unenthusiastic actions lead to unsatisfactory results.'

He also discovers that success is not a constant and has different connotations for different people; only individuals can define, judge, or verify it for themselves; no one from the outside can. Others only see what the individuals unintentionally display through their actions, attitude, and behavior.

In my fifty-year career, I have met many brilliant people who could not succeed beyond a point because they did not have these skills. I dedicate this book to these wonderful people who are always 'highly valued' but not good enough to make it.

I also dedicate it to all my '*gurus*' – teachers, bosses, peers, subordinates, customers, suppliers, contractors, friends, and my lovely family – who shaped my experiences and taught me everything I know today. This book is the essence of those learnings.

All names, situations and characters in the book are fictitious and have been created to balance the flow of the story and its messages. Any familiar name, situation and or character is purely coincidental.

Organization Chart (Partial)

Mastery Function, The Global Company, Inc.

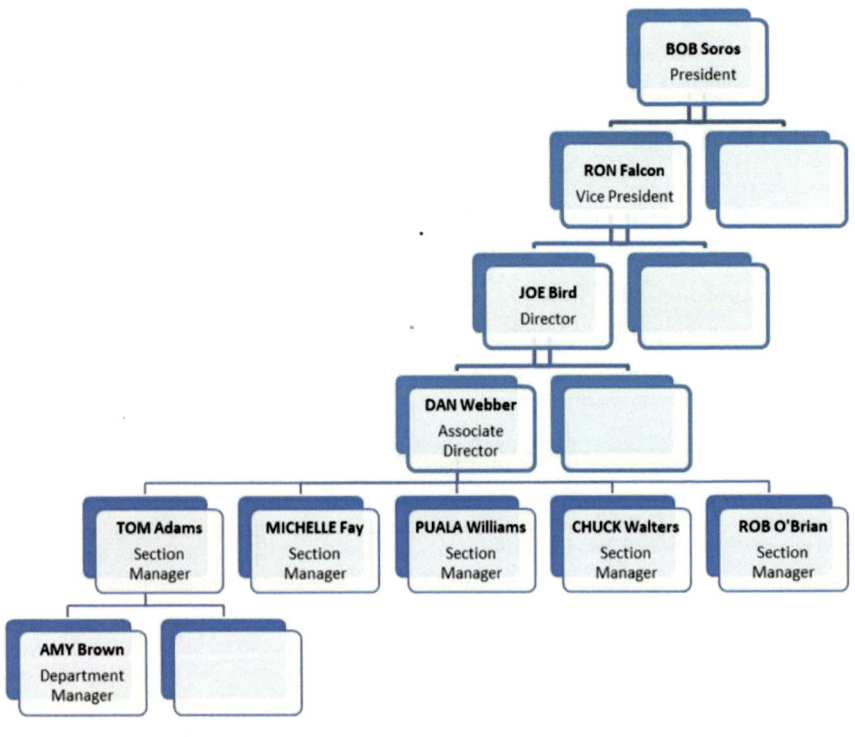

CHAPTER ONE

Thousands of people work in The Global Company, Inc., a great multinational corporation. Tom Adams is one of them. He is a brilliant individual – intelligent, hardworking, and full of energy. There is almost nothing that Tom cannot accomplish. His results are always one of the best. The company recognized his talent by moving him up the ladder three times to section manager level in a record five years, which typically takes ten years for most others. But things have slowed since; he has been section manager for the past four years with no signs of upward mobility.

Tom works in the Mastery function of The Global Company. His function is responsible for end-to-end systems of the company. Unlike the commercial functions, where greenhorns soar and are either allowed to fly higher or shot down rapidly, the Mastery function values experience and technical proficiency, and allows managers to continue their careers at any hierarchal level.

Tom is a valued employee, as his manager Dan Webber always tells him. But Dan is unable to satisfy Tom with this recent stagnation. The reasons, though copious, seem hollow and superfluous to Tom.

Dan is in a similar situation himself. He has been a 'highly valued' associate director for the past six years. And whenever he asks his director, Joe Bird, he too gets a similar unconvincing reply. The key difference is that Dan has already reconciled to the fact that he will not grow beyond associate director. Tom, on the other hand, is still too young and has moved up too fast in the past to accept this sudden stagnation.

Privately, Dan feels dissatisfied about his inability to promote Tom, but is helpless. The talent development system of The Global Company mandates every senior management promotion to be discussed and approved by the leadership team of one-up manager. Dan must gain alignment to Tom's promotion in his boss Joe Bird's leadership team that includes Dan and his peers, Joe's direct reports. Tom's promotion proposal always results in a mixed response in Joe's leadership team. Some always 'but' the proposal, "Tom is good, but…" The 'buts,' though somewhat different have a common theme. Dan cannot understand the real reasons behind the 'buts' and is unable to obtain approval to promote Tom.

Hundreds of managers regularly get the 'but' in The Global Company.

TWO

Dan Webber was hired by The Global Company nineteen years ago through the customary annual campus recruitment. A handsome young man with athletic built, good academic record, and charming disposition, Dan was one of the two hired from his university that year.

A lot has changed since. Although age has made little difference to his looks and physique, the cheerful demeanor has been lost somewhere on the way. It has been replaced by a cold, no-nonsense, controlling attitude with a shade of negativity.

Dan is a technical expert and good at what he does. He made associate director after thirteen years of excellent service. But that was possible only through the strong advocacy and sponsorship of his current vice president Ron Falcon, who ironically was hired by Dan fifteen years ago.

Dan had selected young Ron Falcon through campus recruitment. With an excellent academic transcript, strong extracurricular record, and an attractive personality, Ron was the top pick from his campus. As a trainee, he displayed quick learning and extraordinary leadership skills. He was identified as one of the best new hires and put on the fast-track. Dan's training and coaching played a significant role in the development of Ron's technical knowledge and skills in those early years. He was given roles of increasing responsibility rather early in his career and rose through the ranks faster than Dan. One day, he became Dan's boss.

It was sometimes whispered that Dan is more intelligent, and Ron's bypassing Dan was talked about as an example of the unfairness of the talent development system in The Global Company. Despite that, Ron has good relationships with almost everyone, including Dan.

Dan has a habit of noting observations in his personal diary. He picked this habit up in childhood through his father's encouragement and continues it after forty years, albeit digitally now. He often refers to his notes and finds them the best way to experiential learning. For the past few years, the observations are often about Ron and his exponential growth. The notes often end with a question mark. Dan wonders, *'How can Ron continue to grow?' 'What does Ron have that I don't?'* A satisfactory answer always eludes Dan. He has made several hypotheses but is unable to put his finger on any specific one.

Everyone knows that Ron is exceptionally smooth with bosses and peers, and almost never confronts, to a fault. But Ron is equally smooth with his direct reports and other juniors. He is approachable and genuinely cares for people. In short, he is liked by all, and almost invariably gets his way through with bosses, peers, and juniors.

Dan has thought of asking Ron directly several times in the past but has always hesitated because of the personal and sensitive nature of the question. The bouts of frustration have continued and have started to affect him and his work. During one of those exasperated moments, Dan finally decides to take it head on and approach Ron.

He called Linda Fernandes, Ron's executive assistant, and set up an appointment for Friday evening. He chose Friday purposefully so that he could reflect on their discussion over the weekend. Dan felt much calmer after that and went about the normal day routine.

THREE

Ron came out of his workstation to greet Dan as he walked into his office and hugged him effusively. He guided him to the corner sofa where steaming hot Starbucks coffee awaited them. They sipped coffee, exchanged pleasantries, and began talking about their families.

"How are Betsy and Jonathan?" Ron enquired.

"Betsy is busy with her newfound passion for social work. Jonathan spent the long weekend with us. He is overly excited and is doing well at Carnegie."

"How is Nancy? Is the pregnancy progressing well?" Dan asked.

"It's not great. Nancy's mother is with us now, which has made it easier. The doctor says the first few weeks are the toughest part; she should be fine after that. We are looking forward to the second trimester." Ron replied.

They continued to discuss their personal lives for some more time, and then Ron said, "Linda told me that you have something to discuss, but before we get there, I need some help Dan."

"There have been some complaints since John Carpenter took over the logistics department. Some key performance indicators also show a dip. I chatted with John earlier this week; he believes that the people capability is quite low. I don't get it. Everything seemed fine just a few months back when Ralph Decker was leading. How can the organization capability change so quickly?" Ron wondered. "Will appreciate your thoughts as you have handled that department before."

Dan was quick to respond, "I can't say for sure, but I think the root cause may be work process changes that were implemented just before Ralph was transferred. Leadership change, immediately after such an extensive process transformation, is not advisable as the team is still learning the new procedures. John needs some external support until he learns not only the new processes, but also about his new department and team members. I would suggest bringing Ray Homme on a short-term assignment to support John as Ray has already implemented these new processes successfully."

While talking, Dan was thinking of the question that has been nagging him. *'Boy, he doesn't even know such simple things! What really makes him succeed and grow? But he does seem to value my opinion. I am glad he asked; I can help.'* His thoughts were abruptly interrupted as Ron started to speak.

"This is helpful. I was confident that you would be able to guide me. I will talk to John and see how to help him." Ron's words worked wonders to lift Dan's somber mood and he thought, *'I do enjoy meeting Ron; he makes me come alive!'*

"Thanks again. Now tell me how I can help?" Ron enquired courteously.

Dan hesitated and started rather nervously, "Ron, a question has been bothering me. I thought that you would be the best person to answer it as it pertains to you. I must clarify that please feel free to say no if you find it too personal. I would also like to seek your forgiveness in advance if you find my assertion unnecessarily provocative or rude."

"We go a long way, Dan. You hired me and taught me so much. You are one of the architects of making me who I am today. So, nothing you say will ever offend me. Please be as open and forthright as necessary. I will try my best to answer."

"Thanks. I know I can count on your help." Dan paused and slowly resumed, "I have still not been able to understand why I cannot make director. Although I do not understand or agree, I have reconciled to the fact that I will most likely retire as associate director." He paused. "I see several people making directors who are junior to me and honestly, not as competent. I always wonder what I could have done differently to be one of them. I only see them smooth talking their way out of difficult situations. Their results are not as good; they are not better at identifying and developing solutions or new ideas. I do not see them as better performers, but most certainly there is something that keeps driving them up."

Ron was listening attentively and waited for Dan to finish. He smiled and politely said, "I guess I too am one of them." It was a statement, not a question. He paused briefly and continued. "Before I attempt to answer your question, I have a small query – do you find anything good in us?"

"First, I must admit that yes, I do see you in this group. And yes again; you have several admirable qualities— all of you present very well. You know how to manipulate the data to make your point; and I say it in a positive way. You are persuasive and are mostly able to get what you want. You don't confront even when challenged or threatened; instead, you find a way to rationalize."

"Is there anything else?" Ron was very polite in his probe.

Dan thought for a while and added, "Yes, there is. Everyone, including me, likes you. In fact, it is always genuinely nice talking to you."

"Why do you think that is, Dan?" Ron inquired gently.

"You make people comfortable, I guess. I do not feel

threatened even though you have bypassed and moved ahead of me. I cannot recall any time when you unfairly pushed us to do anything. In summary, you are a good leader."

"Could that be the reason why I and others of my 'tribe' have been moving up?" Ron queried.

"That answer has eluded me for so long and is actually the reason for me to come to you today, but I guess this could be a reason."

"It probably is, but there are few others. I doubt, however, if I can answer your question sitting here today. I hope you will not mind if I try to answer it over time. I will ask Linda to block my calendar every Friday at the same time for the next few weeks if that is okay with you?"

"I would love it. I do realize that the answer is not that simple, Ron. Otherwise, all of us would have got it. Thanks for your offer and the time you will spend helping me. I really appreciate it"

"It will be my pleasure. If I recall correctly you used to write your observations regularly. Are you still doing it?"

"Yes, I do."

"Great. Then I have a request for some pre-work prior to our meetings. Please record your observations and learnings during the week. I would like to review them with you and use them to find the answer to your question. Are you game?"

"I certainly am. Thanks again for your time. I look forward to seeing you next Friday," Dan said.

"You have a nice weekend and say hello to Betsy and Jonathan. By the way, I will inform Joe that I need some personal help from you and will be seeing you every week for the next several weeks." Ron smiled and added, "I don't want him to start speculating what is going on behind his back."

"Also, thanks for your advice on John."

"See you next week. You too have a nice weekend. I hope Nancy overcomes the pregnancy issues soon. Thanks again."

Dan walked out of Ron's office. He heard Ron calling Linda on his way out.

Although he still did not have the answer, Dan was feeling calmer as he reached his workstation. His mind, however, was not on work and was still reenacting the discussion with Ron. He wanted to sit and reflect quietly. He cleared his desk quickly and walked to the parking lot.

Dan was lost in thought while driving home. His first surprising observation was that he did most of the talking; instead of Ron answering his questions, he was answering Ron's. He suddenly realized that Ron does this almost all the time; he always asks simple questions and listens carefully.

'*He made me feel valued,*' Dan thought. '*I am not sure if he really needed or will actually implement my advice on John, but it felt particularly good to be asked.*'

Reaching home, Dan found that Betsy had still not returned. He made a drink and walked into his study to debrief. He booted his laptop and started recording his observations. It took him a long time and several iterations to finally feel satisfied.

Dan's Notes— June 20, 2011
   Observations from my first meeting with Ron Falcon
   1. Ron made me feel valued; he always does.
   a. Ron immediately stopped working as soon as I walked into his office and greeted me like a close friend. It felt good.
   b. He still remembers my likes; it felt great that my favorite coffee was brought.

c. He still remembers my family and their personal situation.
2. Ron made me comfortable that allowed me to open. He always does.
   a. It was a nice gesture to ask my advice on John. It made me feel valued and allowed me to relax prior to the difficult discussion.
3. Ron did not give me any solutions or sermons. He allowed me to do most of the talking. He listened attentively.

As Dan read what he had typed for the nth time, he began to wonder how he would have behaved if he was in Ron's place.

1. I would have greeted the individual from my desk and would have requested him to wait for a few minutes until I finished what I was doing. I am so busy these days.
2. I would not have thought of getting coffee from outside even if I knew it was his favorite. Whatever he needed, I would have asked my assistant to get from the pantry.
3. I would never have sought advice from a junior employee even if I were facing a huge problem; it would make me seem uncertain and weak.
4. I would not have bothered with personal questions and immediately got down to why he wanted to see me.
5. I would have figured out a logical explanation to his question, rationalizing my rapid upward growth.

Suddenly he froze.

'Would I have made my visitor feel the way Ron made me feel? NO! Not even close.' 'My visitor would have felt neither valued nor comfortable. He would have had to hear my monologue and would have walked out probably feeling even *more frustrated than he did when he walked in.'*

The realization came as a shock.

When Betsy walked into the study and said hello, Dan came out of his slumber, unsure how long he was sitting there dumbfounded.

"Hi Betsy," is all he could mutter in a feeble voice. Betsy said something, which he did not hear; his mind was busy drafting the next entry for his notes. "I will join you in just a few minutes. Need to finish this important task." He uttered vaguely.

"Okay. I will be in the garden," said Betsy and walked out. Dan opened a new file, and his fingers began moving on the keyboard.

Dan's Learnings
What Makes Ron Succeed?
1. The ability to make people feel VALUED.

He sat there looking at the screen.

When he finally got up, he was unsure if he wanted to join Betsy in the garden.

FOUR

Dan Webber married his school sweetheart, the stunningly beautiful Betsy Moore, immediately after completing college. They were the perfect couple and almost inseparable in high school. But the choice of university forced them to settle for a four-year long-distance relationship. Dan chose engineering at Purdue and Betsy chose social sciences at UC Berkeley. They decided to get married as soon as they finished college and kept their promise.

After several blissful and exciting years of marriage and parenthood, their relationship began to drift. Both felt it and were unhappy about it, but neither knew the cause or how to avert the slide; oblivious to them, their egos had gained control. Both made halfhearted attempts at rapprochement, but in vain because neither ego was willing to let go. Despite their strong mutual desire to revive the relationship, both put the onus on the other to take the lead, which neither did. The relationship slid further once their only son Jonathan left for college. Although they coexisted civilly and courteously under the same roof, they had little to talk about, and whenever they did, it was only the necessary and mundane.

Betsy had watched Dan transform into a different person who seemed distant and preoccupied; even when with her, he was not there. She was extremely dissatisfied but could not comprehend the reasons for this change. Reluctant to take the lead herself, she silently and painfully watched the gap widen.

She eagerly hoped and waited for Dan to initiate reconciliation; from her side she was determined to respond with excessive enthusiasm whenever he would. But he never did, and she waited.

Dan too was in a similar state; he was waiting for Betsy to initiate. But this weekend was different. His new learnings had made him question himself and think hard. Several thoughts kept intertwining themselves and continually stayed in his head throughout the listless weekend.

Topmost was a revelation that these learnings could be equally useful in his personal life. *'I must practice them with Betsy. How? We have grown so far apart. Can we ever bridge the gap? Do we even care for each other? Can I break this vicious cycle?'*

He spent a long time pondering but even after several agonizing hours, he was unable to figure out a solution, though, one thought had crystallized in his mind.

'I value my relationship with Betsy far more than anything else. I must act to change the current impasse.'

He realized after hours of internal deliberations that a preplanned intervention may backfire as it may seem insincere and could harm instead of help. He figured that situational spontaneity will probably be best as it will come direct from the heart. He committed to doing it at the earliest opportunity.

Dan's frustration grew as Sunday night approached because he had still not found any suitable moment. Though in bed early, he hardly slept. He finally got out of bed around five a.m. His turning and tossing must have woken Betsy.

"Why are you up so early?" she asked drowsily irritable.

Dan's usual instantaneous sarcastic response in such situations was replaced by quiet hesitancy and the words, when they came, startled even him.

"...Because I want to make breakfast for you today." Dan could not believe he said what he just did! *'Spontaneous all right. Boy, what was that?'* But a faint smile broke on his lips. *What a change forty-eight hours have made!'*

Betsy was awake instantly as if jolted.

"You will do 'what' for me? Did I hear it right? Are you all right?" Her rapid questions were like automatic weapon fire.

"I am absolutely fine, Bet," he said using her pet name after eons. "I have been thinking for long that I must lighten some of your burden; Jonathan's going to college and your extended involvement in social work must have put considerable stress on you. I know I have been a little insensitive so far..."

Betsy was out of bed and hugging him even before he completed his sentence.

"I don't know what has got over you Dan Webber, but I love it. Thanks."

They held each other tight. Dan slowly whispered, "Thanks for taking such good care of me and the house despite your current mental state and workload. You go back to bed; I will call you once breakfast is ready." He gently led her to the bed, made her sit down, and quietly walked out of the bedroom, leaving happily shocked Betsy behind.

Dan left for the office after finishing a leisurely intimate breakfast with Betsy. A smile refused to leave him throughout the journey as he reflected on the morning. He was pleased with himself for being able to use his work learnings to make Betsy so happy; he was filled with an unfamiliar energy that he had never experienced before. It was exhilarating!

'How could I have missed this before?'

'Can I use it at work? How and where should I start?'

He thought of Tom Adams. *'These learnings will immensely benefit Tom too.'* He realized. *'Should I try to recreate the Ron experience with him? That will probably be the right start.'*

The thought broadened his smile. He reached the office and was about to call Tom when Michelle Fay, one of his other section managers, walked in.

"Morning Dan. I am glad you are in early. We have a crisis!"

"Morning Michelle. What happened?" Bitterness creeped into his tone as he was about to protest this unplanned intrusion. But his new learning calmed him down as quickly. He paused, smiled, and said, "Michelle, before you blow me away, let's walk to the pantry and get a coffee. It must be serious as I have never seen you in the office this early," he added.

Michelle was taken aback at Dan's response for two reasons. First, she could not recall Dan using small talk before. He would typically jump straight to the point almost invariably; no beating around the bush for our Dan! The second reason was even more surprising. It seemed to Michelle that Dan was not aware of the issue.

'Why? I emailed the details to him last night!'

Dan had the reputation of being one of the most arduous email users in the company who took great pride in clearing his inbox, almost live!

'What has happened today? Something is not right here!' Michelle thought.

"It seems you did not get a chance to see my email on this issue. I was up till late last night expecting your response." Michelle said, trying to catch up with Dan as they walked towards the pantry.

Dan was equally surprised; the thought of clearing his emails, a routine every weekend, did not even cross his mind over this unusual weekend. He was just too busy discovering and experiencing his new learnings!

There was a brief pause as Dan cherry-picked his words, "I am really sorry Michelle for missing your email and keeping you awake so long. I was tied up last night and this morning with something rather important and did not get a chance to look at the emails. Please fill me in." Dan was pleased with his word choice.

Dan's 'polished' response surprised Michelle even more, but she tried not to show it. *'I am sure something is going on. This is not our dear Dan!'*

"Over a million *Evershine* shampoo caps got rejected because of 'flashing' (rough edges). We have no more caps; the supplier also has no stock. The earliest we can get a new supply is the day after tomorrow. So, we cannot produce and deliver the Walmart order that our CEO has committed."

'This is not good.' Dan thought but made sure that his face stayed expressionless. They made coffee in silence, both in their thoughts and walked back to Dan's workstation.

Dan was dying to jump straight to the issue and find a solution but had to make enormous effort to control his instinct. Instead, he said, "Let us get to the problem as soon as we finish coffee. I suggest we walk to the shop floor and see it firsthand. You may also want to ask Purchase and Quality Assurance to join us. Hopefully, they will be in by then."

A conflict was developing inside Dan between his 'usual' and 'new' self. He kept reminding himself, '*I must try my best to use my new learnings and instead of giving the solution, I must encourage my people to get to the solution through my questions.*'

When Dan and Michelle reached the production line,

Production Manager Rob O'Brien, QA Manager Paula Williams, and Purchase Manager Chuck Walters were waiting for them.

"Hey guys. Good morning. Hope you had a good weekend. What do we have here?" asked Dan.

"The caps have flashing. As some of the flash is hard, it can hurt the consumers while opening the bottles. Although the probability is moderate, it is a chance we cannot take," Paula explained without any preamble, the usual Dan-way! She also showed Dan some samples.

Before Dan could respond, Rob jumped in, "Apart from the consumer risk, these flashes are also affecting packing line productivity."

"Thanks. I understand. What about the bottles? Any issues?" inquired Dan.

"Bottles are within the normal tolerance," replied Paula. "No issues there."

"Do we know the root cause of the issue, Chuck?" Dan asked.

"Not yet. The supplier is working on it," Chuck said. "The earliest we can get the next batch is after two days as all the molding machines are tied up with other products from our company. The deliveries for those too are tight," he added.

"What is the potential rejection rate? Can sorting be a solution?" Dan asked.

Paula jumped in and replied, "80-90% caps are affected in varying degrees. If we sort, we may probably recover 20-25%, still not enough for completing the Walmart order. Further, consumer risk may remain as some bad caps may go through manual sorting."

"So, sorting does not appear to be an option. Any other suggestions?" Dan asked.

Rob was the first to respond, "We evaluated two possible solutions. The first one, while an option theoretically, is not practical. So, let us not talk about it. The second option is to manually shave the flash from each cap. This will be very tedious and a labor-intensive job but is probably the only way to deliver the company commitment."

"Any other possibilities?" inquired Dan. No one responded.

"Thanks for this innovative idea, Rob. Key question is can we make it work? Do we have enough hands to do the manual work?" Again, no one responded.

"Is everyone aligned that this is the best option, and we must give it our 100%?"

Seeing the nods from everyone, he added, "Let us go with it. Rob, as most of the work is in your camp, is it okay if you lead this?" Rob nodded.

"Chuck, I am sure we will urgently work with the supplier to prevent recurrence."

"Yes. We will do that," Chuck confirmed.

"Great. Let us get on with it. Please keep me informed."

Dan walked away and all of them looked at each other curiously as they had just witnessed the most unusual behavior from Dan. *'Something wrong with him'* was the thought on all their minds though no one said anything; there was no time for gossip right now. But they were all pleasantly surprised at the finesse with which Dan had handled the situation. *'He listened to us!'*

As he walked back towards his workstation, Dan too was immensely pleased with the outcome and thought he used his new learnings well.

'The old Dan would have called them all into his meeting room, reviewed the situation and pronounced his judgment:

1. Keep the packing line running by sorting good caps.
2. Force the supplier to alter their production schedule and urgently make new Evershine caps.

This sudden plan change would have created a lot of stress not only at the supplier's but also within our organization. And the risk to the Walmart order would have increased due to unpredictability of plan changes.'

'What did I do differently? I did not decide for the team. I made suggestions but allowed my team to make decisions. In short, I valued them – I probed, I allowed them to use their creativity and I listened. We came up with a better solution!'

And his final thought was, 'In the process, I empowered them. Wow! I must do more of this. It feels so good.'

As soon as he reached his desk, he pulled out and booted his laptop. He was surprised as he had never entered in his notebook at work. 'But this cannot wait,' he said to himself. He opened the page where he had summarized his findings yesterday and added one more sentence.

Dan's Learnings
What Makes Ron Succeed?
1. The ability to make people feel VALUED. This EMPOWERS them and produces better decisions/ solutions/ results.

Pleased with himself, Dan went back to work.

The week passed faster than usual. Things were better at home; Betsy was delighted with the new Dan. So were Dan's direct reports who were noticing a difference in Dan's behavior. He had suddenly become collaborative and being with him was not so taxing! Tom too was noticing this positive change in Dan and had decided that he would talk to Dan to understand the cause.

Dan had one of the best weeks in memory and was excitedly looking forward to his second meeting with Ron. The Walmart order was delivered on time. He had written a brief email informing the CEO and received a sweet thank you email back almost instantaneously. Mastery function President Bob Soros, Ron Falcon and Joe Bird too congratulated him on the achievement. He had passed all the kudos to the team who too were delighted at the successful outcome, especially because of their personal contributions to resolve the crisis.

Dan's only regret for the week was his inability to spend time with Tom. He was determined to correct it and had set a meeting with him for Monday.

While Dan was eagerly awaiting the next rendezvous with Ron, the rest of The Global Company was looking forward to the weekend.

FIVE

Dan walked into Ron's office, excitement clearly showing on his face. Ron met him with his usual enthusiasm. Once pleasantries were over and they settled down, Ron said, "Congratulations Dan for meeting Walmart's commitment despite the last-minute problem."

Dan was surprised that Ron was aware of the cap problem. He had always believed that only bad news travelled up that fast in the Global Company.

'I had briefly mentioned it to Joe, but I did it in passing, well after the problem had been resolved. I must try to understand how Ron is aware of an issue that was resolved within hours and had no impact on the results,' thought Dan. *'Probably another learning opportunity here!'*

"It was really important for the company to meet this commitment because Walmart would have delisted *Evershine* otherwise; that is why the CEO got involved." continued Ron.

"The team did a great job. I am glad we were able to honor this important commitment despite the challenge." Dan said.

"How have you been? Were you able to record your observations and learnings as we agreed?" Ron asked, finally coming to the subject. "I hope there were some learnings." He smiled.

"Yes, I did. There are significant learnings for me. I must thank you."

"No need to thank me, Dan; learnings are yours. Tell me

what you learned?"

Dan paused to collect his thoughts as he wanted his reply to be crisp. "I learned that when we listen to people and accept their suggestions, it values and empowers them, and produces better decisions, solutions and results."

"Great learning. We will talk more about these later. Any other learnings?"

"There are some minor ones. I will cover them in due course."

"We will today focus on communication. I am sure you have had several trainings on the subject. But as it is the foundation of what we will discuss later, some repeat will do no harm."

"What is communication? Any thoughts?" Ron asked.

"It is the act of sharing and exchanging information, knowledge, thoughts, ideas and feelings."

"Yes, this is how the dictionary defines it. What do you think constitutes communication?"

"Ron, I had considered communication to be read, write, and speak. I knew listening was important, but I always included it within speak. Last week made it amply clear to me that listening is probably the most important aspect of communication. Another surprise learning of last week was about questions; I had never considered questions as a critical part of communication, but I have now learnt that they are critically important," replied Dan.

"To summarize, communication is Listen, Question, Speak, Read, and Write."

"Is it possible to convert it into a picture, Dan?"

Dan got up, walked to the whiteboard, picked up markers and drew a picture.

"Did I capture it correctly?"

"It is a reasonable illustration of what you described. We will shortly see if this is complete. What are the forms of communication Dan?"

Dan thought for some time and replied, "There are two—Spoken and Written. All others are variations. For example, speaking, listening, questioning are the variations of Spoken; reading and writing are the variations of Written."

"Nicely put." He paused, looked at him intently and asked, "Something seems to be bothering you. What is it?

Dan looked at the whiteboard and said, "I made an error in that picture. The center point of that picture should be Listening as it is the heart of communication."

"No problem, Dan; we will fix it later."

"Right now, I have a question. How did you communicate to me that something is bothering you?"

Dan was taken aback. "Ron, I did not communicate."

"Didn't you? Then how did I come to know that something was bothering you?"

Dan was quiet for a while. "Probably through my expressions or body language."

"True. So, do you agree that there was some communication between us? If yes, are there other communication forms beyond Spoken and Written?" Ron inquired.

Dan had to think. "It appears so. Probably there is a third form – Seen."

"Would you want to correct your picture then?"

Dan walked back to the whiteboard and made some changes to the picture.

"Why is Listen in the center?"

Dan thought for a few seconds before replying, "I realized that listening is the heart of communication and most of us are weak at it; we listen to answer, not to understand. So, we start to prepare the answer or the next question while the other person has still not finished; if only we could listen and seek to understand first, many problems could be prevented."

"Very well said. I understand what you mean. But I ask you to think carefully if your picture is complete or if something is missing."

Dan replied after few minutes, "My picture does not show the relationships."

Ron smiled. "Sorry to take you through this exercise. But it is critically important that you understand this well. Communication is the most important reason for individual success or failure; not only in professional but also in our personal lives."

Ron continued, "Let us now go back to communication through expressions and body language. I 'saw' through your expressions that you were not your usual attentive self. So, I 'felt' and 'thought' that there must be something bothering you."

Ron paused, looked Dan directly in the eye and said, "Communication involves all our senses; part of the message is conveyed nonverbally through our eyes, facial expressions, gestures, body language, tone and silence."

"Trained people know this and ensure that their thoughts and feelings are not betrayed involuntarily. In fact, they go a step further and voluntarily use nonverbals to spice-up and strengthen their verbal communication."

"For the untrained, nonverbal communication is involuntary and telltale; expert communicators cautiously look for nonverbal signs as it reveals inner thoughts and feelings, which helps them to grasp the entire and often even the unspoken message."

Dan was listening awestruck as he had just seen a mini demonstration of the concept Ron was describing. "It is an important lesson that no communication training ever taught us. How can one get trained?"

"It comes with awareness and experience. Let us hope that you will understand the concepts today. It is up to you beyond that."

"Let's move on. Your definition of communication completely misses what is of great importance to us – efficacy of communication! Effective communication is, '**The art of using sight, sound, feel and thought to succinctly convey exactly what we want to share.**'

"What is sight, sound, feel and thought? It is not clear."

"Effective communication is the ability to 'feel' the pulse of the people and the situation to 'thoughtfully' use the eleven pillars – compassion, experience, touch, listen, speak, ask, silence, see, show, write and read – to successfully convey exactly what we want to."

"A picture will probably explain it better."

Ron walked to the whiteboard and drew a new picture. "This is the house of effective communication."

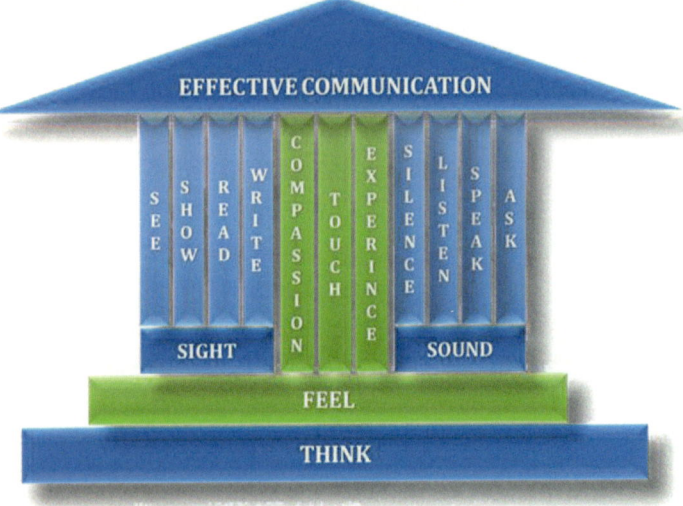

House Of Effective Communication

"THOUGHT is the mind and FEEL is the heart of effective communication; both are essential to enhance its efficacy and impact. 'Feel' creates the awareness and understanding and 'thought' brings coherence and mindfulness."

"Though intuitive that a thought is an essential first step, 'Think' is an oft-forgotten part of the communication cycle. This 'given' is often neglected and communication starts without 'Think', leading to either communication problems and misunderstandings, or ends up being ineffective. The practitioners who understand the importance and priority of 'Feel' and 'Think' are more effective and have less conflicts." Ron explained, looking keenly at Dan as he listened attentively.

There was silence for a while that seemed like eternity before Dan responded, "I guess I fall in the same category. I did not think of it earlier, but I now realize that it was not only 'questioning' and 'listening' that I have been practicing. I also practiced 'Feel' and 'Think' and that made me a more deliberate and effective communicator." "Actually, not only communicator, but an even more effective leader," he added hastily. "Every time I spoke, there was purpose behind it and that was only possible because of my 'Think' before communicating!"

"This is fantastic," said Ron and smiled. "Effective communication is the most important weapon in the armory of a leader. It is also our least understood and weakest skill."

"SIGHT covers the pillars of 'read' and 'write.' We will not talk much about them here as there is enough literature on these subjects. The other two pillars of sight are 'See' and 'Show.' Do you have an idea what they could be, Dan?

"I think they would be what we discussed sometime back, the nonverbals. 'See' is when I observe the nonverbals in others and 'Show' is when I enact them for others. Is that correct?"

"Absolutely! Worthwhile to reemphasize that every conversation is a relationship between speaker and listener; both shaping it. We will miss a critical part of communication without observing the nonverbal signs of the speaker. And on the other side, be aware that listeners too are watching us for these signs; so, we must use nonverbals judiciously to enhance the impact and effectiveness of our communication. This is the reason why face-to-face communication is most effective."

"Coming to SOUND, the first pillar we should discuss is soundless – 'Silence,' which is an effective and under-leveraged aspect of communication. It is not easy though; choosing when to speak and when to remain silent is an art that comes with experience. It requires maturity and control (of ego), specially amidst provocation and incitement. Thoughtful silence can prevent many arguments and conflicts."

"Amazing! I have never thought of Silence as a communication pillar. We have always discussed Speak and Listen," exclaimed Dan.

"Dan, thanks for leading me to the next aspect of sound. Although most of us are not good listeners normally, we become exceptionally good listeners sometime. Have you seen it? What do you think makes a bad listener a good one suddenly?" asked Ron.

"A lot depends on the speaker, I think. Are they talking about a subject that interests me? Are they speaking in a way that interests me? The speaker also matters."

"Exactly, our self-interest and an appealing narrative are essential for active listening. The speaker, though, does not matter; the speaker's reputation and importance may force us to 'pretend-listen' just to show respect, but active listening will only happen if they speak on a subject, and in a way that interests and appeals to us. This requires the speakers to think carefully about their audience. What may interest them and what will be the best way to engage them – and tailor their content and style."

"Have you ever been put off by someone who is pretending to listen to you?"

"Yes. It is such a belittling feeling when that happens; it is as if I am being insulted! It is so upsetting that often I try to end the conversation abruptly. Why do people do that?"

"It happens when people 'think' they already know 'what is being said.' It also happens when what is being spoken either does not interest them or meet their expectation. As I said earlier, conversation is a relationship, and the speakers too have some responsibility for such listening behavior."

"This is clear and makes a lot of sense to me. Could you please also elaborate on 'Ask?' There is a general belief that questions are asked only to pull an individual down or kill a proposal."

"Most certainly. I am glad you 'asked.' Yes, it is often true. Instead of seeking and learning through 'Ask,' we often use questions to display our ego -- our position, power, or knowledge. But it need not be this way. Pertinent questions are particularly important in effective communication. Well-thought-out sincere questions open the door to knowledge and understanding. They can also offer a different perspective."

"Question or 'Ask' is probably the most potent and misused aspect of communication. It's use determines if the communication becomes threatening and defensive, or open and effective."

"I can never forget my induction to the power of 'Ask.'"

"I was invited to make an important proposal to the previous CEO a few years back. After working and reworking the proposal several times myself and with my bosses, I sent it to him for pre-reading. I was invited to meet him after a few days," Ron said, reminiscing.

"I still remember that meeting vividly; all Bob did was to ask me simple questions in such a 'non-threatening' and 'knowledge-seeking' manner that I enthusiastically shared everything without making any attempt to defend my proposal on which I had spent so much time and effort. The questions and their tone convinced me that Bob is a supporter and is genuinely seeking to learn more about my proposal. Before I knew it, I was saying, *"Bob, I would like to reevaluate my proposal and come back to you."*

He looked at me passionately and said, *"Any time. Thank you for so much hard work on this proposal. I will look forward to our next meeting.""*

"Bob's questions had opened new doors for me; it had

suddenly become apparent to me that there were other possible ways to approach my recommendation. Although he was not an expert on the subject, his questions made me, the expert, rethink and realize that there could be different and probably better ways to get to the same endpoint."

"It took me four weeks to re-evaluate and re-analyze all aspects of my new awareness and learnings. I was delighted with my new revised proposal that offered a better solution—lower capital expenditure and shorter lead-time. I sent the reworked proposal to Bob, and it was approved within twenty-four hours without the need for me to see him again. That is the power of effective Ask."

Dan was listening to the story mesmerized. Before he could say anything, Ron continued. "I spent lot of time analyzing that meeting with Bob that created such learning and knowledge for me. I categorized Bob's questions:

"Probing questions to seek clarification or challenge and validate assumptions.

"Why questions to discover the root cause of a problem.

"How questions to explore different routes to a breakthrough.

"Coaching questions to help visualize what else is possible.

"I narrate this story to give you the flavor, Dan. Communication is such an intriguing, but immense and challenging subject that it is almost impossible to make any concluding statement; one is constantly discovering and learning new things."

"It is time to now look at the flow and relationships of these pillars." Ron walked to the whiteboard and drew a new picture. "To make it simple, I have color coded these. Orange is 'feel' and 'think,' green is 'sound' and blue is 'sight.' What do you think of this?"

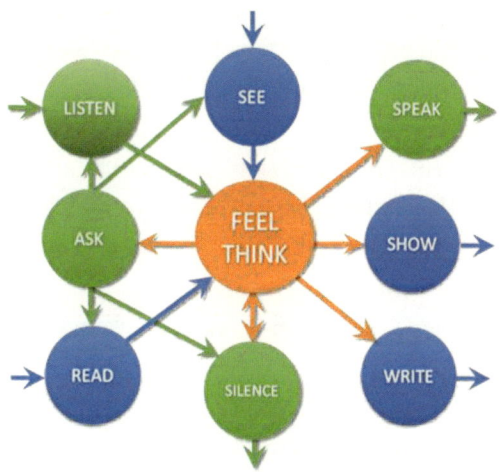

Effective Communication Linkages

Dan said, "This picture is extremely helpful. I am beginning to see communication challenges much more clearly now. It is surprising that communication is considered to be all about language proficiency. How can we educate and train people on these concepts?"

Ron answered, "The basic concepts are not that difficult, and most people know them; some important nuances are perhaps misunderstood, and different people probably interpret them somewhat differently. The real challenge, however, is not ignorance of the concepts, but of practicing them; inconsistent practice is what makes it difficult and challenging. I do agree about the need for education and training though, around 'think,' 'feel,' 'nonverbals' and 'ask.'"

Ron paused, allowing Dan to assimilate this very crucial message, and then added, "Now that you understand the concepts, I am sure that you can practice them. Remember, it all begins with 'feel' and 'think!'"

"I am now much better equipped and committed to practice them consistently," Dan said.

"Before we end today, I want to go back to something you said a while ago which is rather important," Ron said.

Dan seemed lost; he could not recall what he had said that could be so important. His expressions said it all. Looking at him, Ron smiled and added, "If I recall correctly, you said something, and I paraphrase, 'language fluency is considered the yardstick of good or bad communication.'" Seeing Dan nod, Ron continued, "You have unknowingly raised an important point, though about a slightly different angle of communication; about challenges of cross-cultural communication that adds a new dimension to what we have discussed so far. A few examples will help you understand this better."

"In China, where English skills are rather low, it was very difficult to assess the communication skills of the applicants because the interviews were conducted in English. We were unable to determine whether poor communication was because of English proficiency or lack of skill. We thought of a solution and started requesting local Chinese co-panelists to ask a few questions in Mandarin. The purpose was to assess how well they communicate in their mother tongue. It was not surprising that the communication effectiveness of many candidates improved dramatically as soon as the foreign language barrier was removed. We selected them. More importantly, we also found several who still communicated poorly. We rejected them."

"A global company like ours communicates in the global language, English. Everyone, irrespective of their ethnic heritage or location, communicates in English; some are fluent in English, others are not. We focus on understanding the 'intent' of the communication rather than on the 'exact meaning' of 'each word' while talking to people from 'low-English-skill-countries' like Japan or China; we accept that their choice of words is not deliberate due to poor English proficiency. On the other hand, when we communicate with nationalities that are English fluent, we follow the normal practice of focusing on the 'exact meaning' of 'each word.'"

"I have found this to be a potential cause of misunderstandings. '**Language fluency does not mean cultural congruence**'; people use English words differently based on their cultural background. Let me illustrate with a simple example."

"What does 'couple of them' mean to you?"

"It means a couple 'two people or two similar things. It is pretty simple," replied Dan.

"Probably not that simple. Most people in Asia use 'couple of them' not only to represent 'two' but can also use it to represent 'few.' If you were talking to someone in Asia and they used this expression, there could be misunderstanding if you are not careful."

"I have found that we must be more cautious talking to non-native 'supposedly fluent' English speakers and must vet their words with the filter of their cultural background; especially with someone who is not very well known to us."

"Very interesting," murmured Dan. "I never thought of this; no wonder I got into some misunderstandings with my Indian section manager, Ramesh Parekh. Can face-to-face communication prevent these misunderstandings, Ron?"

"They are unconnected, Dan. But face-to-face can help in certain situations. For example, nonverbals (gestures) came to our rescue whenever we relocated to a non-English-speaking country."

"I guess you would have used written communication like email far more than verbal as their written English capability is much better. Right?" Dan asked.

"Not really. Allow me to answer this more broadly as you have raised an important question. Communication is a two-way process and remains incomplete in email format until the other party has responded. People often assume that they have 'communicated' by just sending an email. This is a common fallacy as we cannot know when, and whether our email has been read fully and understood correctly. 'Sending' of an email is only the first part and is premature to assume that communication has happened! In fact, some people exploit this weakness of email format and intentionally use emails as data-dump just to claim, 'I already informed you'."

"Let me ask you, Dan, if you have to inform me of something urgent or need my quick decision, would you send me an email or would you want to call or meet me face-to-face?" Ron asked.

"I would prefer to meet face-to-face because then the communication is more effective and instantaneous. Calling you would also be an option because although the communication may not be as effective, it is still instantaneous. Email will be my last choice because I will never know if you have read my email," replied Dan, recalling Michelle's disappointment when she realized that Dan was ignorant of the Evershine cap issue although she had 'communicated' it clearly in an email.

He paused and asked, "Ron, are you suggesting that we should not use emails?"

"No. Email is a very important communication tool; it gives us the ability to share data and detailed documentation that the receiver can review at his or her pace.

"An email, however, must be preceded or followed by a

phone call or face-to-face meeting if alignment or approval is required. Second, sufficient time must be provided to the receiver to review and digest the data. Third, the email subject line should clearly articulate the purpose of the email, for example – For Info, For Approval, For Alignment etc. Finally, email text must be short and crisp. All these points are absolutely essential for emails with large data or documents. Short, crisp and clear emails communicate effectively, are read fully, and responded quickly."

Ron looked at his watch and said with a smile, "Dan, it is quite late already. I do not want to keep you away from Betsy on a Friday evening. I am sorry our session became so long today, but we would have lost the rhythm by splitting communication over two sessions. I hope you found it useful."

"Thank you, Ron, for your patience and time. This has been an eye-opener. I have attended several communication trainings, but they are typically focused on better writing or speaking. What you explained today may seem rudimentary and mundane, but I can clearly foresee that it will make a huge difference if I can practice it! I feel so privileged that you gave me so much of your time. Have a nice weekend." They shook hands and Dan got up to leave.

"Thanks Dan. But, before you go, I want to leave you with one last thought on communication."

Dan halted and looked up at Ron who was speaking with a quiet smile on his face, "**What NOT to say is even more important than what to say**! Think about it." He paused for a few seconds to allow it to sink in and continued, "Have a nice weekend, Dan. See you next week. Say hello to Betsy."

Dan walked out of Ron's office with excitement on his face. Even Ron's last-minute shock-therapy was unable to dampen his feelings. He did not want to waste even a minute before summarizing today's thoughts. *'I must capture them before the weekend chores get me,'* he thought.

While walking toward his office, he called Betsy.

"Hi Bet. How was your day?" He listened to her enthusiastic response. When she finished, he continued, "Sorry, I am still in the office. Something important has come up."

Before Betsy had a chance to protest, he added, "How about we go to your favorite restaurant tonight? I can meet you there in an hour."

"No problem, Dan. Would love to. See you there soon," Betsy said cheerfully.

He smiled to himself sensing the happiness in her voice, but more because he had caused it!

He booted his laptop and started recording his thoughts.

SIX

Dan and Betsy were having a wonderful weekend. Dan had already told Betsy that he would need to spend Sunday afternoon working on an important project. He wanted to reflect on the new learnings and crystallize them into workable action steps.

Unlike the past, Betsy did not complain as she was really enjoying the new Dan, who had become more understanding and caring; probably for the first time after their marriage he was listening to her, and they were truly communicating. She did not know what had caused this welcome change, but she did not want to probe for the fear of breaking the spell. *'It is fine if Dan wants to take the Sunday afternoon to himself; the more important thing is that now he is with me whenever we are together. Unlike the past when he was physically with me, but his mind was somewhere else!'*

After a lazy brunch with some close friends, Dan and Betsy returned home. Dan had been with her all weekend. They had a wonderful time at Betsy's favorite restaurant on Friday night, spent almost the whole day at the golf club together on Saturday and watched a concert at night. It was one of those rare weekends that Betsy dreamt of. They had not had such a good one in years.

"I hope you don't mind my leaving you alone for few hours, Bet?" asked Dan.

"Not at all, Dan. This has been one of the most pleasant and enjoyable weekends I have had in years. You go ahead and finish your work. I will see you at dinner," Betsy replied and walked to her bedroom.

Dan went to the kitchen, took out a chilled beer can and moved to his study. He closed the door as he walked in. Beer in hand, he turned on his laptop and moved to the notes he had hurriedly made on Friday evening.

Dan's Notes June 27, 2011
  My Second meeting with Ron Falcon
  1. It was a learning experience. I had never considered communication this way. *I need to do lot of work on all the aspects.'*
  2. **'Feel' and 'think' are the starting point, holding nine other pillars of effective communication. Silence and other nonverbals are so important.**
  3. 'Ask' is an extremely important, but misused aspect of communication.
  4. Most of us are weak in 'listen'.
  5. Communication is a two-way process and is not complete until the other party responds. Email etiquette needs to be learned and taught.

Dan sat deep in thought, Ron's meeting running through frame by frame. As he completed the replay in his mind, he realized that he missed the question Ron had posed in the end. He quickly added another point to the list.

  6. Good communication is not only what to say, but also what NOT to say!

'Let me start by reflecting on this first. This is an immensely powerful reminder that words, once spoken, cannot be retracted. A wrong word or sentence can cause irreparable damage to a situation or relationship, especially if the other person is not very

well known to me and may not seek clarification.'

He was suddenly reminded of an Eastern proverb that his friend, Karan Chopra had recently told him, *"Words can cause deeper wounds that hurt more and heal far slower than the wounds of a knife."* He had not thought about it then, but it started to make sense now. *'This further amplifies the importance of 'feel' and 'think' in communication.'*

Dan's Learnings

What makes Ron Succeed?

The ability to make people feel VALUED. This EMPOWERS them and results in better decisions and solutions.

The ability to communicate effectively. He starts with FEEL and THINK, ASKS to learn, LISTENS to understand and uses NONVERBALS well.

Feeling satisfied with his notes, Dan closed the laptop and went to the kitchen to help Betsy with dinner.

After a long and relaxed dinner and quick clean up, they sat in the garden with a bottle of their favorite wine, talking about things they had probably not talked about for years. Even more noticeable was the intense intimacy with which they talked; it was like two close friends meeting after years, wanting to make up for lost time!

As the full moon leisurely lit up the night sky, they too gathered themselves and slowly walked to the bedroom, hand in hand.

SEVEN

Reaching the office on Monday morning, Dan found Tom waiting for him. He had requested Tom to meet him before the day-to-day routine caught up with them.

Although he had been noticing a change in Dan, Tom was still surprised when Dan greeted him with uncharacteristic passionate enthusiasm.

"Hi Tom. I hope you had a great weekend. Sorry that you had to wait."

"Not a problem, Dan," is all Tom could say. He was still busy thinking about Dan's changes.

As they settled down, Dan asked, "How is Tara? Did she take the GRE test?

'Family Talk! It is deeper than I had thought.' Tom thought to himself.

"She is doing good. She chose to postpone GRE and her PG plans as we have finally decided to start planning a family," Tom said with a hint of a smile.

"Wow! That is fantastic news," Dan said. "You will never regret this decision. Bringing up a child is the most beautiful experience of life. Please tell Tara to call Betsy if she needs any guidance or help."

"Thanks. Will do."

"What did you want to see me about?" Tom could no longer control his curiosity about this meeting request from Dan.

"Over the past few weeks, I have been pondering over your

question that I have always brushed aside. I may still not have all the answers for you today, but I am beginning to see what you will need to do to make associate director."

Dan started to summarize all his learnings of the past two weeks. He shared everything except his meetings with Ron; he thought it was neither appropriate nor necessary. *'There is no need to show my weakness and that I am seeking help,'* he thought.

Tom heard him but was not 'listening,' wondering if this is the new diplomatic way to say why I cannot be promoted. Although he wanted to give Dan the benefit of doubt, this thought constantly bothered him.

'Is Dan prepping me up for the next performance review? How convenient to convince me why I can't be promoted even before the results are reviewed!'

"Well, Tom. I do not want to keep you any longer. You have a busy day ahead. We will meet again and continue our conversation."

Dan, who was now aware and conscious of nonverbal communication, decided to cut short as he had begun to sense that though Tom was physically here, he was not with him.

'Very surprising. I am sharing with him such important learnings, but his mind is somewhere else. Probably he is preoccupied with something else,' he thought. *'Anyway, I will catch him later when he is more relaxed.'*

As Tom left, Dan's phone rang, and he immediately got involved in the business of The Global Company. The clock on the wall smiled and beckoned 9:00 a.m.!

Dan was busy throughout the day and the morning meeting with Tom just slipped out of his mind until he sat in the car to return home.

'Why did Tom not respond enthusiastically? Why did such important learnings, which are changing my life, not interest him? Was he preoccupied or did I fail to engage him? I thought I used all the right tricks to start. What did not work?'

Dan's newfound commitment to work and family kept him fully occupied through the week and left no spare time to himself, but his 'failure' to engage Tom lingered as a dull pain. What he thought would really excite Tom had fizzled, but what really concerned him was his inability to pinpoint the reason. The unanswered 'why' bothered him constantly.

Driving back from work on Thursday, he received a voice message from Betsy.

"Sorry, darling. A school friend just popped up after twenty years. So, we decided to meet over dinner. Your meal is in the kitchen; just warm it up. Feel bad to leave you alone, but I know you will understand. Love you."

He did not want the communication to remain incomplete, so he stopped the car by the side and punched the keys in his cell.

"I am delighted that you are meeting an old friend after so long. Have a great time. I will be fine. Take care," he texted ending it with a thumbs up. He pressed send.

Realizing that he had the evening to himself, his thought again wandered to the meeting with Tom and the question 'why.' Reaching home, he parked the car in the driveway and entered through the kitchen. He warmed the food, pulled a chilled beer from the refrigerator, and walked to the study. As he sat down, he again went into the 'why land'.

'Why did Tom react in such an indifferent way? Why couldn't I excite him? I had used all the tricks I have recently learned.' And suddenly it hit him...

'Tricks! Why have I thought of this word more than once? Was I really trying to trick him? Into what? No. I was not trying

to trick him into anything. I genuinely want him to get the same learning as me; I am his well-wisher. But, if I thought of this word more than once, is it possible he too may have felt that I was trying to trick him into something? What? Acceptance of his non-promotability? But what may have prompted him to feel this way? Did I say something that may have given that feeling? What?

He started to replay the whole conversation in his head.

'I started with 'build rapport,' asking about his family. I 'listened' to him. I then explained the learnings which I had carefully thought through (think). I allowed him to ask questions... Wait, he did not ask any! Oh my god, I was unable to engage him! But why?'

'Did I explain why I wanted to meet him? No, I did not. Neither did I share how I acquired these learnings. I just started preaching. Yes, it must have sounded like preaching! In absence of the context, Tom must have been confused about the purpose of our meeting. Yes, that is it. I should have told Tom about my meetings with Ron. Why did I withhold this important information? Was it my insecurity? Providing the context could have helped Tom understand my intent and prevent any suspicions. In absence, Tom must have tried to guess the reasons why I was doing what I did and may have probably reached the wrong conclusion.'

He realized that he had finally found the 'why!' He pulled out his laptop, opened his learnings file and started writing.

He read it again; the screen reminded him of the botched-up opportunity to engage Tom. The food and beer remained on the table, untouched

EIGHT

Dan reached Ron's office full of anticipation for another exciting session but was surprised to find that Ron was not there. Before he could ask, Linda was by his side explaining, "Ron had to rush for an urgent meeting, Dan. He asked me to tell you that he is sorry that you will have to wait. I should have called you and postponed the meeting, but I did not for a selfish reason." She looked flushed as she said that. Dan noticed the steaming Starbucks from the corner of his eyes. He asked, "How can I help, Linda?"

"It is rather personal and sensitive, but I know that I can trust you." Her voice went down two notches as she continued, "I have a major dilemma, Dan. A headhunter has approached me with an excellent opportunity outside the company; although the role is similar, the salary is far more attractive. However, The Global Company is such a good company and Ron is such a nice and caring boss that I can't make up my mind. It is such a pleasure working for him; he is understanding, considerate and fun to work with. I have never been so confused before. Unfortunately, I cannot consult him. I would really appreciate your guidance?"

Dan stayed quiet, nervously thinking how to respond to this unusual situation. People had asked his opinion on personal subjects earlier too, but this was rather bizarre as she was his VP's executive assistant.

Despite Linda's eager looks, Dan did not want to rush into an answer. Using his new-found-knowledge on communication, he wanted to feel and think first. But he could not continue to stay quiet and had to say something, *'I will have to think on the fly, so I must start with preliminaries.'* He thought to himself.

"Linda, I feel honored that you chose to confide in me on such a personal matter. It is difficult for me to give you a straight answer. Moreover, it is a matter on which only you can make a decision." He paused and tried to look in control, but internally he was flustered and was thinking feverishly what to say next. Suddenly it flashed, relaxing him. He made sure that his external composure remained unchanged.

"Do you know the two most important reasons for people to leave a company?" As Linda nodded in the negative, he continued, "salary or compensation is not one of them; the first is 'relationship with direct boss' and the second is 'visibility of and confidence in career plan.'"

"The reasons are simple – a direct boss can make work life either exciting or hell. And a clear career plan energizes and inspires the individual. I do not know if you have visibility of your career plan, but I know that you have a fantastic relationship with Ron. In case you have still not discussed your career plan with him, you easily can; this visibility will help your decision making. Finally, before you decide, I suggest that you talk to Ron." He paused, thought for few more seconds, and added, "Not sure if I helped Linda, but I doubt if I can do any better." Dan concluded feeling satisfied with his handling of the situation.

"Thanks Dan. This is extremely helpful. You have given me enough to mull over. Thanks so much," Linda said.

Just then Ron walked into his office. "I am so sorry Dan that you had to wait. There has been a crisis and I had to attend an urgent briefing."

"Not a problem, Ron; I understand. Is there anything I can

do to help?" Dan inquired.

"Not right now. I will certainly come to you if something is needed. Let us get back to our subject." Ron sat opposite Dan after picking up a paper from his desk.

"How was your week?" he inquired.

"If I were to summarize in one-word, it would be exciting. There is a new viewpoint and I see situations differently now. What you explained in the past two meetings is not new; I have read and heard almost everything in bits and pieces. But you have given me a new perspective. These 'known' pieces have fallen in place like a completed puzzle that makes so much more sense now! Thank you for that."

"You are welcome," Ron said referring to the paper he was holding in his hand, "I am so glad you think so. However, let us now crystalize what we talked about last week which will prepare us for today's topic."

"Recall I asked you the purpose of communication last week and we discussed the theoretical aspects then. I now want to explain how successful people use communication. But before that, I must ask you another simple question: what is influence?"

Dan thought briefly and replied, "To me, influence is getting people to do what you want them to do."

"This is good but let me ask you another question. What is the difference between persuasion and influence?"

Dan was silent. The second question made him think harder. After a while he added somewhat hesitantly, "I think persuasion is logic or a data-based push to get something done. Influence, on the other hand, is the external force that evokes internal desire to do it."

"Well said, Dan. The key difference between the two is rather simple. I can persuade you through my position of power or my superior knowledge or logic and data, but I will never be able to inspire you. I may also not be able to gain your personal commitment. My persuasion may get the results, but it will be because that is your job and because you know that the company expects you to perform." He paused for a while and then continued, "Instead, if I were to help you understand how the requested actions and results will improve consumers' lives or help us become a green company, it may inspire you. Persuasion may induce obedience to the instructions, but influence will invoke inner desire to act. Persuasion is short-term while influence is long-term. Results achieved through persuasion may neither be as good nor may provide you the same level of satisfaction that results through influenced inspiration do."

Ron continued, "Your definition of influence was right, but only partially. Although most will sign up for it and this is how they practice it too – we make people do what we want them to do. And they do it because of our power – power of hierarchy, power of age and experience, power of perceived knowledge superiority or power of emotional blackmail. Key word being 'power.' We use our power to make them do it through persuasion NOT Influence."

"What your definition missed is just one word, but that one word turns the concept of influence on its head!"

Ron said, "True and meaningful influence that unleashes inspired action and delivers extraordinary results comes not from 'getting people to do what you want them to do,' but from **'getting people to WANT to do what you want them to do.'"**

Ron paused and saw Dan's expressions transform from 'I-know-it' to 'passionate-quest' at the simplicity, yet potential for enormous energy this small change in definition could release. He smiled and continued, "It inspires and excites people to listen, understand and follow. Every great leader, be it India's Gandhi, China's Mao, Africa's Mandela, or America's King understood this and were able to influence millions to create revolutions! And effective communication is the only means to true influence." Ron concluded and smiled again.

There was a long pause as Dan sat there almost frozen and then said in an animated voice, "Ron, communication has suddenly taken a totally different dimension for me. It has also become clear to me why we spent so much time on it last week."

"I am delighted you feel this way, Dan. For today, this will be our focus…"

While Ron was still talking Dan thought of his conversation with Linda just a while ago. *'Was I able to influence Linda to make the right decision or was I persuading her with logic and data to stay in the company?'*

Ron's words brought him back.

"The issue is not finding persuasive data or logic or arguments to push our point of view; we are always equipped with loads of it and love to throw it around. The real challenge is our ability to inspire and excite people to do what we want them to do. Data or logic by itself seldom inspires people; it can persuade, but not influence."

Dan's whole career flashed past him as he sat there motionless. *'Persuading is what I have done throughout my career. And not only at work, but also in personal life!'* Ron's voice again brought him back to the room. As he refocused, Ron was standing at the whiteboard drawing a picture.

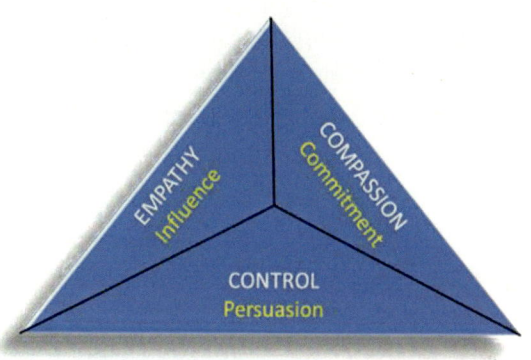

"We typically parade the power of organization chart or our bio or our knowledge to gain **control.** We prevail over individuals and direct them to do things they may or may not want to do. Only **persuasion** comes from control."

Ron paused for a while and then continued, "**Influence** happens once we begin to **empathize** with the individuals, and it changes their attitude, behavior and actions."

He paused again, "But an even higher operating level is **compassion**, which emanates from a feeling of concern for the people we care about, accompanied by a strong desire to help, and benefit them; it builds trust and strong **commitment**. We typically do this with our family and close friends. The challenge for us is to grow our triangle of compassion and empathy to encompass all those we work and live with or meet. This cannot be achieved without conquering self-interest and personal ego and diminishing the need for power and control."

A thought flashed in Dan's mind, '*Ron is putting so much time and effort to help me only out of compassion.*' He had to quickly return to the real world as Ron was still speaking.

"You may have noticed that I used the word 'diminish' for power and control; I did not say eliminate. This is because there are situations when power and control may be essential. For example, regulatory compliance and consumer quality are mandatory and may require certain levels of control. Similarly, control, persuasion and handholding may be necessary until an individual or a team achieves the desired capability. This is also true in case of parenting; parents, under certain situations, may exercise control over their children, but it is out of their care and concern for them."

Ron paused and then added, "I want to reemphasize that control may be necessary when the individual or team capability is low." He got up and drew another picture. "This will probably explain it better," he added.

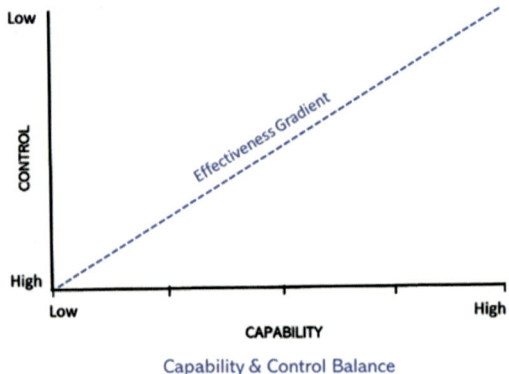

Capability & Control Balance

"We must allow more freedom as the individual or team capability increases; too much autonomy when the capability is low can result in personal/ team failure and loss of confidence. Similarly, too much control when the capability is high can stifle the team and its creativity. Though not difficult once you are aware of it, the real challenge for a leader is to be able to make an accurate assessment of the capability."

Ron stopped speaking, intently looking at Dan and asked, "What are you thinking, Dan?"

Dan was quiet for a while and then softly replied, "Ron this is a particularly important lesson. I have often used control as the key operating style. I was wondering how I will be able to make the change to empathy or compassion?"

"It is not that difficult," replied Ron and with a smile added, "Now that you are aware, you will become conscious. But the more important aspect is to care for the people; empathy and compassion will automatically follow. Genuine care comes only when your concern is selfless. This is important to understand."

He continued, "You may have noticed that some people 'show' they care, but it is for a 'purpose.' This 'selfish show' is neither empathy nor compassion. This falsehood is easily noticeable, and the motives get questioned and doubted."

Listening to Ron, Dan started to think of his meeting with Tom.

'This makes lot of sense. Although I met Tom out of care and concern for him, I was certainly operating from control, rather than empathy or compassion. No wonder Tom felt I was trying to persuade him with some ulterior motive.'

Ron's words pulled him back. "As a final point, because it does not encourage participation, control confines the options and constrains the results as the decisions and actions are based only on the leader's personal knowledge and experiences. Empathy and compassion, on the other hand, broaden our horizon and excite involvement and contribution of others for better decision making and superior results."

Ron looked at his watch. "It is quite late, Dan. So, if you do not have any questions, let us call it a wrap. However, I do want you to mull over one question. Is conflict good or bad? We will discuss it next Friday."

Dan said, "I much appreciate your time and help. This is really fantastic." Unable to hide his excitement, he took Ron's extended hand, thanked him again and walked out of his office.

Linda had already left for the day and was probably still wrestling with her dilemma. Dan would not know.

Walking to his workstation, Dan was thinking about the last part of their conversation. He was ecstatic about Ron's reaffirmation of his analysis about the meeting with Tom. The most satisfying part was that he had reached the conclusion himself without Ron's help. He had already started to picture his next happy rendezvous with Tom.

Instead of waiting in the office, he decided to leave for home so that he could be with Betsy as early as possible. *'There will be plenty of time over the weekend to summarize the learnings,'* he thought.

He picked up his bag and headed towards his car.

NINE

Dan and Betsy had another lovely weekend. The past few weeks had dramatically changed their relationship and had in some ways brought back their younger days. They were once again enjoying being together, to the extent that sometimes even words were not necessary; their silence said it all. Neither of them was willing to talk about the change or its reasons for the fear of breaking this magical spell.

On Sunday evening as they relaxed in the garden with a nightcap in their hands, their eyes had a unique glint of content, satisfaction and laughter that comes only in the company of a very dear friend. From Friday evening, they were constantly together doing almost nothing, except enjoying and basking in each other's comforting company.

Dan broke the spell, "Hey Bet, I need to get ready for tomorrow. Is it ok if I leave you alone for some time? Alternatively, you can join me in the study. You can read something while I finish my work."

"Go ahead," Betsy replied. "I will catch up with my emails and messages. See you soon in the bedroom," she added with a mischievous smile.

Returning her smile, Dan got up and kissed her cheek gingerly, briefly massaging her back. He easily lifted her to her feet and they both walked back into the house.

Dan entered his study with a purpose. He had something very important to figure out. *'What has caused Betsy and my relationship to improve so dramatically?'*

This question had been at the back of his mind ever since, but he was unable to get to the root cause of it. He was not ready to discuss it with Betsy just yet, so he wanted to find the answer himself.

He eased into the recliner and with closed eyes began comparing past the few weeks versus the past few years. Though reluctant to admit it, he knew that 'negativity' had creeped in their relationship. The past few weeks had not only transformed it but rekindled the excitement of early years – the days when they were discovering each other! A certain warmth filled him and made him smile.

His thoughts wandered to his newfound learnings and how he had used them with Betsy. While he could recount everything he did differently, the root cause of this hugely welcome change still eluded him. Understanding the reason for this transformation was critical because he knew that sustaining it would otherwise be impossible. The failures of their earlier attempts were stark reminders.

'Will it help if I first figure out what had gone wrong in our relationship? The answer to my question may probably lie there,' he wondered.

He started going down the ladder of dates but was unable to pinpoint a time or incident that could have been the possible trigger for the woes in their relationship.

'It was a slow drift that probably took several years but accelerated once Jonathan left for college; Betsy and I had little to talk about after that.'

The mental gymnastics was exhausting him. *'Should I first summarize my learnings of this week and then come back to this question? I am stuck right now.'*

He switched his thoughts to last Friday session and Ron's words echoed. "Control confines the options and constrains the results as the decisions and actions are based only on the leader's personal knowledge and experiences" *'Because it does not encourage participation, control constricts our ability and restricts our options and outcomes,'* he thought.

He drew Ron's control-empathy-compassion (CEC) triangle. Recalling Ron's words, he tried to reflect on the model, but Betsy and his relationship question overpowered his thoughts, and suddenly an insightful and eye-opening realization cleared his mental fog.

'Betsy and I were both in control mode! Trying in vain to persuade each other to see things our way.'

Instantly, he was upright with eyes wide open; it was a Eureka moment!

'God, it was not just trying to persuade, we were both jostling to take control.'

He sat immobilized; an intriguing theory had begun to form in his mind.

'Each one of us is in our own personal triangle, a space that houses our emotions, including control, empathy, and compassion. When we get in a relationship, a large part of our personal triangles merge, creating a common and shared emotional space. Empathy and compassion are undefined spaces and both partners can happily coexist there. 'Control,' on the other hand, is a well-defined confined space with room for only ONE person who controls the relationship.'

'Relationships flourish where 'who-will-occupy-control' is obvious and accepted, like bosses or parents in hierarchical relationships. It is far more complicated in relationships of equals— couples, siblings, peers, friends. Sustaining such equal

relationships is challenging; it can be done only if both partners either align and unconditionally accept who takes control or both agree to give up control. Otherwise, both will constantly jostle to wrest control, resulting in unending unpleasantness, conflicts, and possible relationship breakup.'

'OMG! Betsy and I were in this situation of both attempting to seize control and neither willing to cede. This was causing frustration, annoyance, and exasperation for both of us! Our relationship has revived only because we have both vacated control.'

'We have now moved to empathy and compassion – the area of understanding, care, and concern for each other. It has allowed us to value each other; bringing a remarkable tranquility and calmness in our relationship.'

'I think I have found the answer.' But several questions still bothered him.

'Can it be sustained?' wondered Dan. 'Moving from control to empathy was easy and seamless. Wouldn't going back to control be equally easy?' The question frightened Dan and he shuddered in cold sweat.

'I cannot allow our relationship to slide back! We must find a way to sustain it. Understanding how we came out of control may probably help.'

'We dropped our egos. Control feeds on ego; no ego, no desire to control!'

'We have brought our relationship from the verge just in time. We will control our ego and shun control, if not for our, at least for Jon's sake!'

His thoughts turned to Jonathan who has been the glue holding their relationship. Jon, as they fondly called him, was close to both and maturely balanced the relationship without taking sides. Thoughts of Jonathan brought quietude to his mind, as they always did. Dan recalled that even Jon, in his teens, had rebelled whenever on rare occasions they tried to control him.

'With Jon, I generally operate from empathy or compassion; it comes naturally. And that is probably the reason why we have such a good understanding and relationship!' Another check for his theory.

The more he thought, the more confident Dan got of the true reason for the earlier deterioration and the current dramatic improvement in Betsy and his relationship, *'I have root-caused it well.'*

'It is simple yet so difficult to understand. How many relationships can be saved with this understanding? Is it that easy to give up one's ego and control?' he wondered. *'Certainly not easy, but it can be done if one is committed to it. We did it!'*

Another question popped up in his mind, *'When one of the two moves from control to empathy, will the other always follow?'* He did not know. *'Not sure but probably yes. I was the first to move out and Betsy followed almost immediately!'*

Another critical question bothered him. *'What happens if one of us drifts back to control, as it is quite likely? The other must display understanding and patience; and, under no circumstance should try to follow!'* It was not an answer but an aspiration.

'Too many questions. I need to think this through a lot more. It is such a powerful learning! I must find a way to share it with others. It has the potential to save many relationships.'

He relooked at Ron's control-empathy-compassion concept drawing; it looked incomplete and did not capture his new insights. He took a new sheet and redrew the CEC Triangle. It took several iterations before he felt satisfied.

Feeling happy and elated, he turned on the laptop and started correcting the notes he had hurriedly made on Friday evening.

Dan's Notes July 4, 2011

Dan's 3rd meeting with Ron

1. Influence is not to make people do what I want them to do, but to make them WANT to do what I want them to do!
2. I have operated through control/ persuade throughout my career. How can I first move to empathy/ influence on my way to compassion/commitment?
3. People in a relationship must vacate control space to sustain and strengthen their relationship.
4. Control-empathy-compassion can all co-exist. Success is in our ability to choose the right what and when.

He read the points several times, replaying his conversation with Ron.

'This is probably the most valuable lesson so far and this understanding will impact me directly as 'control' is my predominant emotion. I will have to learn to move to and stay in empathy and compassion. Ron said it will come naturally if I can care for people selflessly. Tom's disappointment should be a learning for me. All I needed was feel and thought, and empathy and compassion. As Ron explained, being aware is the key. I must be more conscious until it starts to come naturally. Yes. That is probably the right approach.'

He quickly summarized his new learnings and realized that he must also edit the previous ones as his understanding had broadened.

Feeling satisfied with his edits after a few corrections, he saved the file, closed the laptop, and looked at his watch. He was shocked to see the time; he had spent far too long.

'Betsy must be waiting.' He quickly got up and almost ran out of the study.

He silently walked into the bedroom feeling terrible for being late. He found his bedside lamp on and Betsy asleep wearing his favorite nightie that revealed more than it covered. He adoringly looked at her accentuated curves and flawless tanned skin that looked even more sensuous in the soft light of the night lamp. *'Gosh, she is so beautiful!'* he thought as he stood there undecided whether to wake her or quietly go to sleep.

Without opening her eyes Betsy whispered, "You back? What time is it?"

"Sorry, Bet. It is late; I lost track of time."

"Not to worry, Dan Webber. You come here and better make my wait worthwhile," she said with a suggestive smile.

Dan slid next to her, held her tightly and kissed her full on the lips. They slowly explored every part of their bodies, gently and unhurriedly, enjoying every touch and caress. Each giving, trying to pleasure the other selflessly, till they fell asleep in each other's arms. Even the clock on the wall had lost track of time.

Dan's eyes opened a few hours later. *'What was that! Did we have sex?'* He wondered. *'No! It was divine; we made love.'* He went back to sleep. The smile on his face was of a man who had found the only oasis in a vast dreary and arid desert after days of wandering in hot summer.

TEN

Betsy and Dan overslept as the morning dawned lazily fast. While aware of the time, they were too cozy to get out of bed. Reluctantly, Dan got out as he had scheduled a meeting with Tom. He kissed Betsy lightly and whispered, "Morning, Bet. I must go as I have an early meeting. You take your time."

Betsy opened her eyes, smiled, and kissed Dan back. "I too am getting up, darling. You get ready while I fix the breakfast."

Reaching the office, Dan found that Tom was not there. After waiting for a while, he called his intercom, but there was no answer. He waited some more. When Tom still did not show up, he sent him a message. Tom replied immediately.

'Sorry Dan. Fell ill suddenly. I emailed you last night that I will not be able to make it today.'

Dan re-read the message and a sudden rush of anger triggered his ego. He had stopped checking emails on the weekend for the past few weeks. He knew that this change is already being talked in the office and Tom should have been aware of it.

'How could he do this to me? I am sure he knew I would not read the email on the weekend! Has he done it intentionally? Is he avoiding me? Why?' Anger, following its proven role to perfection, was overpowering his ability to think.

'Did our last meeting upset him so much?' The thought suddenly calmed and moved him out of control to empathy. *'He is certainly disappointed. I must find a way to influence him to*

see me.'

He sat at his desk motionless thinking of various ways to manage this situation. He stayed that way for a long time until Anita interrupted, "Dan, time for a meeting with Bob."

The rest of the day and week passed at a furious pace. The office and home kept Dan too busy, and he did not get time to either think of or meet Tom.

Friday evening arrived faster than usual. Dan was getting ready to go for his meeting with Ron when his mobile rang. It was Linda.

"Hi Dan, hope you had a good week. I want to catch you before you come here. Thank you for helping me make the right decision. I have decided to ignore that job offer..."

"Yippee," exclaimed Dan, not allowing her to finish, "This is fantastic news, Linda. Your leaving would have been a huge loss for the company." He could almost hear Linda's big smile. "I will see you in a minute."

Walking towards Ron's office, he thought of the satisfying difference between old and new Dan. Old Dan would have used these same words, but at the wrong time to persuade Linda when she asked for his advice last week. Their impact would have been dramatically different. Instead of the inspirational complement that Linda heard now, the same words would have been heard as an attempt to persuade her to stay, eroding the objectivity of his advice. *'The amazing power of effective communication,'* he thought to himself.

He smiled at Linda as he reached Ron's office. She returned an even bigger smile. No words were necessary.

Ron was waiting for him. After the pleasantries, Ron asked, "Any learnings, Dan?"

"Yes. I had a Eureka moment. I realized that when people

get into a relationship, their individual spaces merge into a shared common emotional space that comprises of control, empathy, and compassion. Relationships thrive in empathy and compassion space as both partners can coexist there with trusted influence and selfless commitment. But control space is different; it has place just for one person and evokes egoistic persuasion. For a relationship to survive, the partners can choose to either leave it vacant or accept who will occupy it. Trouble starts when both jostle to take control of the control space. The consequent conflict wrecks the relationship."

Ron was listening awestruck, "This is a highly insightful learning, Dan. I had not even thought of it. To the best of my knowledge, no one has explored this angle before." He paused with his eyes fixed at some object beyond Dan.

"Profound! I like it a lot." He murmured deep in thought, and then smiled like the one who just found something highly valuable, "You have discovered the probable root cause of most relationship failures, Dan."

"Thinking aloud, control constricts and firewalls our domain, not allowing the other to enter without jostling, as you describe it. When control is exercised in relationship of equals, it awakens their ego to fight back."

"I very much like your description of limited shared space between two people in a relationship that both jostle to take control."

"When we allow others to enter, our sphere expands and transforms control and persuasion to influence and commitment through empathy or compassion."

He stopped and smiled again. "Original and immensely powerful thought, Dan!"

Dan had been thinking of something else, *'Am I not seeing*

another winning skill of Ron – he admitted that he had not even thought of this concept. He could have easily maintained the aura of being the all-knowing big boss by claiming he was aware. I would have accepted it without a question! By recognizing and excitedly appreciating my 'original' thought, Ron not only demonstrated his integrity, but he also valued me and elevated me to the position of a teacher. Boy, it feels wonderful!'

Seeing Dan in deep thought, Ron too had paused.

"Thanks, Ron. It feels great to be recognized. I like the way you have recast my thought; it makes more sense. I took the liberty to convert this concept into a model," Dan said and put a sheet on the table.

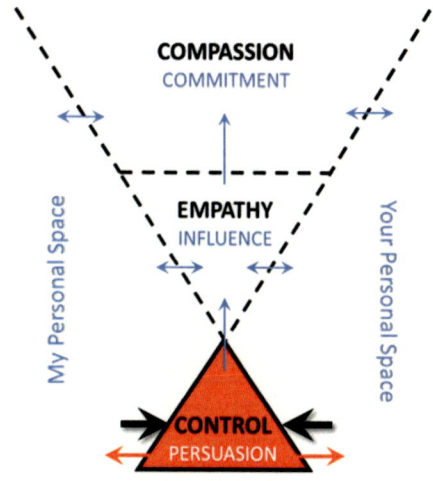

"Very interesting," said Ron studying the model. "It vividly captures your concept – the blocked control space with room for only one individual and one-way flow of persuasion, porous empathy space for people to move in and out and influence flowing either way, open compassion space with no limitations and commitment for all."

"You have well captured a significant aspect – though tough, we can choose to move from control to empathy and compassion. My only suggestion is to show it as two-way flow because the undesired reversal, from empathy/compassion to control, can happen easily and involuntarily."

"Well done, Dan. I love it." Ron said with admiration in his voice.

Dan was elated, "Thanks, Ron."

"I am sure you look forward to our sessions Dan, but what you may not know is that I too look forward to our sessions. Do you know why?"

Dan had no clue, and it was visible. Looking at his blank expression, Ron continued, "You have engaged me by not only being attentive during our sessions, but by your enthusiasm to learn, interpret, understand, and apply these learnings in real life. This is fantastic and is also giving me learning opportunities."

"Thank you also for helping Linda make the right decision on her own without persuading. It is a great example of expanding your sphere and allowing Linda in."

It did not surprise Dan that Ron was aware of Linda's conversation. He knew how easily people open up to Ron.

"I used my recent learnings, Ron. The credit should go to you."

Ron just smiled.

"Let's start today's topic. Were you able to reflect on my question of 'Is Conflict good or bad?'"

"I must apologize, Ron. I was so excited with my discovery of the control-empathy-compassion, CEC model, that I forgot about the homework." Dan said apologetically. His thoughts again comparing old and new Dan!

'Old Dan would have never admitted that he missed a

deadline and would have cooked up an off-the-cuff lackluster response that would have done more harm than good. *Boy, am I learning fast!'*

"Not to worry. You did far more than the homework. You created a brilliant model – but the name CEC does no justice to it; let us call it **Dan's Triangle of Relationship** – a model that relationship counselors may use for generations to come!" Ron smiled flatteringly.

Dan sat there not knowing what to do or say other than imagine Dan's Triangle of Relationship being taught in Jonathan's class at Carnegie. The thought lit up his face despite his best effort to conceal.

"Okay. Let us start with conflict definition. Conflict begins when **'wants are mutually impossible'** between two individuals, groups or even nations."

"Can conflict also be within an individual, Ron?" Dan interrupted Ron.

"Dan, you have once again gone ahead of me," Ron said smiling. "By traditional wisdom, a conflict requires more than one want involving more than one entity. Let's call it external conflict. But as you rightly point out, conflict can also be within— the internal conflict. Dilemma is the mildest form of internal conflict. War is the severest form of external conflict."

"Ron, while you call dilemma the mildest form, it can be the most exhausting and devastating as we cannot get away; it is within." Dan again interrupted.

Ron nodded his approval with his trademark pleasing smile, "Yes, internal conflict is difficult to manage and very destructive if not managed well; it can lead us to shrinks! Let us address it first."

"Almost all management books focus on external conflict."

He paused, "While internal conflict is mostly incarcerated in psychology books. We will cover it first because it can consume us and apart from all the psychological ramifications, it often interferes with our ability to make the right decisions. When before the event, it can cause analysis paralysis; and remorse and decision-fright in hindsight!" Ron paused again for Dan to absorb the thought.

After a brief pause Ron asked, "What do you think causes internal conflict?"

Dan thought for a while. "Indecision, I would think." "It happens to me whenever I have too many options."

Ron smiled again, "It is close. Options are not the real problem though; we can sift through them and choose what we consider to be the best. It may take time, but it gets done eventually."

"Internal conflict begins when we fret over our decision or our response to a situation."

"As you may have heard, Dan, our life is defined not by what is thrown at us, but by how we respond to it." Ron paused, "Instant reaction may indulge our ego but will most likely cause retrospection. Once we 'think,' we begin to wonder did I respond right?"

Dan had moved into his own world. *'Internal conflict has caused me numerous hours of retrospective agony. Should not have done that or said that? What if I had done this or that?'*

Being aware that Ron was looking at him, he pulled himself back and found his voice, "Yes, this has been a cause of concern for me. I often retrospect and wonder were my actions and/or words appropriate? Could I have done something different? What if I had done or said this or that? It is very draining!"

Ron was listening intently. He gently nodded in agreement

when Dan finished and observed, "It is instinctive to wonder if I could have responded in a better way; this is assessment. The challenge, however, is in learning to prevent inconsequential retrospection. Assessment and retrospection have commonality yet are different. They review the same situation, but assessment focuses on how I could have been more effective; retrospection cries over spilt milk with frustrating 'what if' replays. I will explain this in more detail later." Ron paused again allowing it to sink in.

Ron could sense that Dan was thinking hard. "What do you think is the solution, Dan?"

Dan stayed quiet for a while, thinking, and then added, "The only solution could be what we discussed earlier. We had identified 'feel and think' as the first step of effective communication; our action too is a form of communication and 'feel and think' first should apply here too. When we take time to feel and think, we can tailor our response, which is not possible when we respond instantly."

"Excellent," Ron remarked. "Very well said. Every situation gives us the opportunity of choice between a negative or positive response. But the choice only becomes evident when we wait ThERe (**Th**ink, **E**valuate, **Re**spond). ThERe is particularly important when something disturbs, angers, or agitates us. Without it, we can create space for our ego to take control."

"A learned person once told me, never give into the urge to respond instantly to an email or message if it irritates, annoys, or infuriates you; it will be your ego talking! Write your reply immediately to vent if you must, but do not press 'send'; instead, put it in your draft folder. Read it again when you are calm; you will invariably change that draft to make it more balanced or just delete it."

"Same is true for our actions or verbal response. Unfortunately, there is no draft box in a conversation or situation. ThERe is the only way to prevent our 'ego-act' and respond mindfully. It is challenging but can become instinctive through awareness and practice."

Dan was visibly pensive, *'So true. I was ego-acting with Betsy until a few weeks back; not surprisingly I felt bad instead of happy whenever I said or did something to get the better of her. And each time the retrospection cycle started.'*

"Let us talk about external conflict now. Recall we agreed that conflict is 'when the wants of two entities are mutually impossible.' What is the difference between want and need?" asked Ron.

Dan, who was still with the previous thought, interrupted, "Sorry, Ron. I have a doubt. Appreciate if that can be clarified before we move on. You mentioned the difference between assessment and retrospection. I got that but I am wondering where 'introspection' fits?"

"Excellent question, Dan! I should have covered it. I must warn you though that my interpretation goes beyond and may probably be inconsistent with the traditional or the dictionary."

"First, both introspection and retrospection are intrinsic. Although both happen within, intro looks at or into one's self, retro looks at or into the past."

"Second, introspection inspires conquest of indecision and indiscretion, allowing us to think clearly and act mindfully. Retrospection rues the past and degenerates into frustration and perplexity. We can choose either, as both choices are continually available to us. Intro leads to the positive path of inspiration and action, retro to negative path of self-pity and inaction. Does this make sense to you, Dan?"

"It certainly does. Thanks."

"To answer your question about the difference between want and need." Dan paused for few seconds and continued, "Want is desire, while the need is inherent. For example, food is my need as it is essential for my survival, but my want could be a certain type of food, cooked in a certain way."

"Again, well-articulated, Dan." Ron complimented. "Let us stay with your food analogy; assume that you and Betsy go out for dinner; she wants to eat the spicy Indian food while you want French. There is a conflict. Are your and Betsy's needs different? Probably not. You both want to have a meal, enjoying each other's company in a nice cozy place. Despite your needs being the same, there is a conflict."

Dan thought briefly and asked, "So, what really causes the conflict, Ron. Want or need? If our needs are the same, then there should be no conflict."

"Good question. Let us see this dichotomy with a rather simple yet the most powerful illustration I have come across."

"Mary and Miranda, twin sisters lived with their parents. One day they both came to the kitchen, each wanting an orange. Unfortunately, there was only one orange left: conflict! The loving sisters that they were, they decided to compromise, shared the orange equally by cutting it into two parts and went about their business happily: conflict resolved. So, it seemed! Not true though if we examine their needs."

"Mary's 'need' was to make orange juice; she made the juice and threw out the rind. Miranda's 'need' was to make orange cake; she ground the rind and threw the pulp."

"Splitting the orange equally appeared to be a good solution till their needs were known. In reality, half the orange was wasted, and they both shared only the other half! Both could have got a full orange if they had gone beyond their wants and discussed their needs – Mary full pulp for the juice and Miranda full rind for the cake. While their wants, one orange each, was mutually impossible because only one orange was available, that one orange could have fully met their needs."

Dan was sitting wide eyed admiring the simplicity yet the power of the example.

Ron continued, "This is what normally happens. We attempt to find a compromise based on 'wants' without trying to understand the 'needs.' Many conflicts can be avoided, and compromises optimized if only we spend effort to understand the need, which could be common. Eli Goldratt, the famous Israeli author, calls it the Common Ground Model."

Dan had begun to think of his conflicts with Jonathan. *'I should evaluate the big ones to see if we too were caught up in wants without understanding the needs.'*

"Ron this is certainly powerful but rather simplistic. What about the conflicts that are beyond the want and need problem?"

"You are right, Dan. Many conflicts can get resolved by understanding the need, but often even the needs can be mutually impossible. The world of external conflicts is rather complex because our 'ego' fuels it. You can read all philosophical texts for ego description, but for me, it is rather simple. Our ego is what drives us towards a 'Win-Lose' solution and most often lands us in 'Lose-Lose' conflict."

"So, what may be the solution if even the needs are mutually impossible?"

"I think compromise is the only solution then," responded Dan.

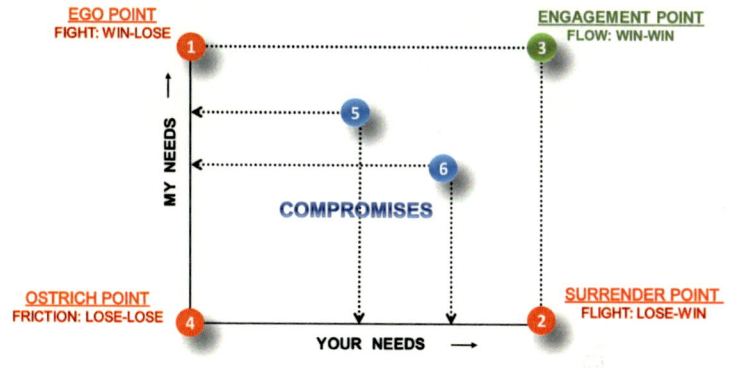

The Conflict Square

"True. The conflict square will help us understand this better." Ron walked to the white board and drew a picture.

"What do you think is the difference between point one and point two, Dan?"

Dan thought for a few seconds before answering, "I think at point one my need is fully met, but no part of your need is met. Point two is the reverse; your need is fully met, but no part of my need is met."

"Absolutely! Said another way, at point one, 'I Win You Lose.'" He paused to create an impact of what he was about to say. "This is the '**Ego Point**' – Not only do I want to win; I also want you to lose. At point two, 'I Lose You Win'. This is the '**Surrender Point**' – I allow you to win. At Point three, 'I Win You Win.' This is the '**Engagement Point**' – both our needs are met. Everything between these points are compromises; some meet more of my needs, some yours."

Listening to this Dan had started thinking how often he gets to the Ego Point in a conflict situation. *'Almost always! Except when it is with Jonathan. In fact, whenever Jonathan wins in a conflict between us, I feel happy. I always get to the win-win engagement point with Jonathan?"* The thought made him happy, but he wanted to confirm his theory.

"Ron, whenever Jonathan and I have a conflict and he wins, I feel happy. In fact, I try to make him win. Isn't this the win-win engagement?"

Ron smiled, "Excellent question that is particularly important to understand. The key is to recognize whether your needs were also met. Often, we sacrifice our needs and allow our loved ones to win. Has that been the case with you, Dan?"

Dan was quiet as he tried to recall past incidents. As he thought of them, he realized that he did sacrifice his needs to meet Jonathan's. It was a revelation!

As Dan spoke, the words came slowly under the weight of this important revelation, "I did compromise my need, Ron. So probably it was lose-win." He paused, took a deep breath, and continued, "But what if my real need is to make Jonathan happy and the conflict was with my want? Isn't that what we really desire for all our loved ones?"

"Another excellent point, Dan," Ron was smiling at the innocence yet the wisdom behind Dan's question. "Management theories typically fall flat when we try to apply them to our loved ones, especially our children. But this is an intriguing angle that I have never explored. Let us do it together." Ron stopped, closed his eyes deep in thought.

"Where do we typically operate in Dan's Triangle of Relationship when we deal with our children?" Ron thought aloud.

"In compassion Ron, even if we move to control, it is out of concern for them not for an ego trip," replied Dan. "But it is also true that I happily compromise my wants to meet Jonathan's; I would not know if our needs were different as I was not aware of this concept then. I can say this for Betsy too – compromising our wants for meeting Jonathan's has given us great pleasure. So far, we have always thought it to be a win-win."

Ron's voice got softer, "Parent-child is a unique relationship without a parallel in our work lives. Why shouldn't our work lives also be this way is a question for another day. Today we must address an unplanned, but extremely interesting question."

"What are we doing by compromising and allowing our children to win? Are we training and preparing them for the tough world outside or are we getting them ready to be hugely disappointed when people in the real-world refuse to compromise and not allow them to win easily? Is it truly win-win?" Ron looked at Dan quizzingly with a gentle smile.

Dan had turned white as if he just saw a ghost. He had always wondered why Jonathan had such a hard time in the first semester of his freshman year at the college. The ugly truth was staring at him now. He slowly gathered himself and spoke in a feeble voice, "Thanks, Ron. Some important things are clearer now."

Ron realized that an internal conflict was brewing in Dan's head as his tone got even softer, "This lose-win conflict resolution is called 'Flight'. As the word suggests, we flee from the situation to prevent confrontation. Does that resolve the conflict though? No. It just postpones it for another day. Retreat may be the right short-term tactic in certain situations, but conflict resolution will still require even more work later. The other thing to ponder," Ron continued, "while lose-win is Surrender Point for me, it is the reverse win-lose Ego Point for you! So, by my flight, I am unconsciously building on your ego!"

Dan started feeling worse with the realization that what he considered help may have instead harmed Jonathan.

Seeing him deep in thought Ron stopped talking and looked at him inquisitively. "Is something the matter, Dan?" he asked.

"No. I have just begun to understand some missteps of the past. Thanks again. The smog of ignorance is clearing."

"Great. Let us move on. The point one ego point way of conflict resolution is called 'Fight'."

"Is it the confrontation that you said is essential to resolve a conflict?" asked Dan.

"No. There is a significant difference. Recall what we discussed that in win-lose I not only want to win, but also want you to lose. Conflict resolution here is by dominating the other – win at all costs! It does not resolve but prolongs or intensifies the conflict. The opponent who might not be ready or is unwilling to fight back now, may choose flight for the moment, to return stronger later. Bottomline, the conflict remains unresolved."

"Confronting in this context is to recognize the conflict and tackle the real issue head-on without either aggression (win-lose ego) or defensiveness (lose-win surrender). Fight the issue, not the individual. The most important aspect is to engage; go beyond the wants to understand each other's needs and evaluate if and what are the synergies. Such engagement can only happen when there is a visible desire to celebrate the differences and explore a common solution. This preferred win-win conflict resolution way is called 'Flow' by management gurus. I call it the engagement point."

Dan, who was listening attentively, interrupted, "Ron, is agreeing to disagree also a win-win conflict resolution?"

"Another excellent question, Dan." Ron remarked, "As we discussed earlier, often the needs of two entities may not intercept or the opinions may be far too rigid. Agreeing to disagree is an effective win-win approach to end a conflict as it allows both parties to neither fight nor flight without compromising their needs."

"Is it clear?" Ron inquired.

As Dan nodded, Ron pointed towards the whiteboard and asked, "What is this lose-lose point four, Dan?"

"It seems to be the worst outcome, Ron. Neither of our needs are met, probably because of either unresolved conflict or a failed resolution. Perhaps a clash of egos as both parties fight it out. This could also be a war situation," Dan said.

"Well said. There could also be other possible reasons. For example, fight-fight or flight-flight. The important thing, however, is that we get here only when a conflict is allowed to persist and simmer; we know things are not right but instead of tackling, we push them under the carpet each time they stick their ugly head out. I call it the **'Ostrich Point'** where we bury our head in the sand, but the friction never ends! And you are right, Dan; this is not the place to be," Ron concluded.

He paused for a while and asked, "We started today's discussion with a question. Is conflict good or bad? What do you think now, Dan?"

Dan was quiet as he collected his thoughts. "It is a tough one, Ron. I would have certainly said bad this morning. Now, I am inclined to call it good because it is an opportunity to engage and improve our relationships, if managed well."

"Well said, Dan" Ron smiled.

"It is quite late; let us call it a day. I will keenly await your learnings next Friday."

He rose and walked towards Dan with an outstretched hand, "Say hello to Betsy and have a great weekend."

"Thanks, Ron. This has been another extremely valuable session. I cannot thank you enough for your time. I look forward to seeing you next Friday. Good night."

They shook hands and Dan left for his workstation, lost in

thought. His immediate concern was to engage Johnathan and find a win-win for an unresolved conflict that had existed for some time. He had so far avoided addressing it, wishing it away but it had not. It had reached the ostrich point and kept coming up repeatedly. Johnathan wants to buy a car and Dan has been persuading him not to. Today's discussion had convinced Dan that it must be resolved urgently.

Dan's dilemma, whether to summarize key points of today's session now or later at home, was resolved within minutes by practicing ThERe. He cleared his desk and called Betsy while walking towards the parking lot.

ELEVEN

Betsy had invited a few close friends for drinks on Friday evening, which was a pleasant surprise for Dan. They had a great time.

Dan had told Betsy that they needed to talk to Johnathan over the weekend. Betsy, though intrigued at the word 'they' just nodded without any comment. They agreed that the best time would be to call him on Saturday afternoon. Johnathan had already confirmed his availability.

After a lazy brunch, they decided to retire to the deck. Dan refilled the champagne glasses and called Johnathan.

"Hi Jon. How are you buddy? I am putting you on speaker as Mom is also here."

Johnathan was surprised because his parents hardly ever called him together.

'Not sure what is going on,' he thought.

"Hey mom and dad. How come you remembered me on Saturday and that too together? What's up?"

Johnathan's comment made Dan and Betsy exchange glances with adoring smiles. "What is going on between us, you will see when we meet," said Dan with an even wider smile accompanied by Betsy's soft laughter.

"Seems exciting! I cannot wait to see what is happening between you two." Johnathan laughed, "When can I come home?" He was genuinely pleased. His parents' visibly strained relationship was a cause of deep worry for him.

Their passionate look at each other deepened their smile. "How about we come to Pittsburgh? Betsy asked with laughter in her voice and an inquiring look at Dan, who smiled and nodded.

"That will be fantastic," exclaimed Johnathan. "Should I book us at Hyatt Place?"

"That sounds great, Jon. Book a two-bedroom suite. You will know what we are celebrating when we meet. We will arrive on Friday next week and leave Sunday afternoon. We will drop you on the way," Dan said.

"You will not need to drop me if you buy me the car that I have been asking for so many months," remarked Johnathan with mild frustration in his voice.

"That is what we want to talk to you about, Jon." Dan quickly responded. "This issue has been with us for a while, and I have been skirting around it. We want to resolve it today."

"I know you want to buy a car and I do not want you to do that now. Our wants are mutually impossible. As I have avoided discussing this so far, neither you nor I know the reasons behind our wants; in other words, what is the need that is driving our want?" As he stopped talking, Dan was not sure how Johnathan was responding to this, but he could see that Betsy was rather amused. *'She has never seen me being so reasonable,'* he laughed within.

There was complete silence at Johnathan's end.

"Let me go first," commented Dan. "Jon, you are aware of my views on global warming. I am reluctant to spend money on another fossil fuel guzzler. More so this new start-up Tesla Motors has developed amazing electric cars and is just a few years away from creating the ecosystem to support their successful commercialization. That is also the reason why mom and I have been using our cars for over three years." Dan looked at Betsy who was looking at him in admiration. "Do you understand my need, Jon?"

"Ya, I get it. Thanks for clarifying."

"My need is not that complicated. I need wheels to travel around the campus. It is so difficult to commute without a car in our 140-acre campus, especially in the winters. I hope you understand."

"I understand. Is Zipcar the solution? Have you tried it?" Dan had prepared well.

"Yes, I have. Zipcars must be picked up and dropped at the same point, East Campus Garage. How do I get to or from there?" Johnathan countered; irritation evident in his voice now.

"You have any thoughts Bets…?"

Before Dan could finish, Betsy interjected, "Now that both your needs are clear, the conflict between your wants can easily be resolved." She waited for the impact and continued, "Jon, would you have an issue with a leased car? What about you, Dan?" She looked at Dan with a flourish.

"Wow!" Jon and Dan said, almost in unison.

Betsy's triumphant expression was priceless. Dan loved it, *'Did I just score two homeruns with one shot?'* He smiled to himself, *'Apart from the win-win resolution of Johnathan and my conflict, I have valued Betsy by allowing her to come up with the solution. Another win-win! You are learning fast Dan Webber.*

"That is a fantastic solution, Bet," Dan said looking at Betsy admiringly and clapping his hands lightly.

"Jon, you go sign a one-year lease for the car you want. Just be conscious of the environmental impact as you choose the cars."

"You made my day."

"And dad, if you don't want to drive next week, take the most environment-friendly solution – train or limo." "I will pick you up and we will have my car to move around when you are here." Johnathan concluded with a delightful chuckle.

They talked for another ten minutes about other things.

After hanging up, Dan and Betsy instinctively hugged each other fondly and kissed. They deserved it for jointly finding a win-win resolution to a conflict that seemed simple but was potentially ominous.

The weekend was moving fast. Unknown to Dan, Betsy had scored two tickets to Dan's favorite baseball game Saturday evening. Thanks to her, the weekend was proving to be one big, pleasant surprise for Dan.

After dinner on Sunday, they followed their new agreed routine. Betsy went to the bedroom and Dan slipped into his study to summarize the learning of the past week.

TWELVE

Monday started uneventfully. As Dan sat in the car to drive to work, his upcoming meeting with Tom was the only thought. He wanted to do it right.

'I hope he will not hang me up today! He has confirmed that he will be there and there is no email either.'

'I must not screw up this time. I must ensure that Tom has complete background and the context of why I am explaining these things. Intent, as I learnt, must be clear to avoid any misunderstanding. But first I must resolve the conflict that has been created by our first meeting.'

Dan walked into the office and found Tom waiting, looking somewhat anxious. *'He is still worried about our last botched up meeting and doesn't want more of the same.'* Dan thought.

"Good morning, Tom" he said, enthusiastically shaking his hand. "Thanks for coming early on Monday morning. I really appreciate it."

"Good morning, Dan. It is not a problem." Tom's tone was polite but had a hint of disapproval as if saying, *'Did I have a choice, boss?'*

"This may take long Tom, so let us get some coffee and go into a huddle room." Dan added. He dropped his bag on the side table, pulled some sheets out and took Tom's arm as they walked towards the pantry.

Once they were settled in the huddle room, Dan looked Tom in the eye and said, "I want to first apologize for the dissatisfying meeting last week. I goofed!"

'Lose-win surrender is the right way in this conflict situation,' Dan thought.

Before Tom could get over the surprise from this un-Dan-like admission of personal failure, Dan continued, "I failed to provide the context and my intent for our conversation that day. I am sure you were extremely disappointed. Sorry for that." Surrender continued!

Tom's anxiousness vanished and a light smile replaced it, "Thanks, Dan. Yes, I was confused as I was unable to understand the purpose. It appeared to me that you were once again trying to justify the reasons for my stagnation."

"I realized that too, seeing your cold reaction to what I thought was a very important discussion." Dan hesitated, took a deep breath, laboring for the choice of right words, "I had withheld important information from you probably fearing that I might seem weak." Dan was aware of the tightness in his stomach as he spoke those difficult words conveying something that he had never admitted to anyone in his life. Though he tried not to show outwardly, the tension in him had raised his heartbeat and suddenly the air conditioning had stopped cooling; his body was hot.

Tom was sitting stunned, speechless and it showed on his face. He had never seen Dan so vulnerable. At that very moment Dan went up a notch in his esteem. Truth and transparency can do this to people. Win-win!

Whether Tom became aware of how he was feeling, Dan did not know. But as the weight was now off his chest, he started to breathe somewhat easier. *'Boy it is not easy to share your vulnerability with a subordinate! But I think I have engaged him.'* he thought.

After what seemed like a long silence, he spoke again, "It is not easy for me, as your boss, to admit that I too have had the same question – Why can't I be promoted?" He paused again, "The key difference is that unlike you I have reconciled to it. But I have promised myself that I will find us the answer to prevent you getting to my situation." He hesitated again.

"I consider you to be a brilliant individual and one of the best at your level. That I have not been able to push your case in Joe's leadership team has been cause of deep frustration and dissatisfaction for me." He paused and took a deep breath.

Tom was sitting across the table with his mouth open and an expression that Dan would never forget. He could not describe it as he had never seen it before.

It took tremendous effort for him to continue, "I went to Ron Falcon with this question, and he has been helping me understand what you and I can do differently. To be clear, I positioned it as my question. I did not want your name in this; you still have a long career ahead of you. What I shared with you last week were my learnings through Ron's help."

Tom's shock and surprise were replaced by something that could probably be best described as gratitude. He tried hard to recall what Dan had explained last week but could not as he was not listening then.

Tom cleared his dry throat and said, "Dan, I must also apologize as I was too flustered and actually did not listen to you. Can you please repeat it for me?"

"I well understand, Tom. The fault is mine as I was unable to engage you. I do plan to take you through the whole learning."

Pleased to see the eagerness in Tom's eyes, Dan started explaining his interactions and learnings with Ron from the very beginning.

Two hours later Dan finished by explaining Dan's Triangle of Relationships and the conflict square. He was mindful of Tom's nonverbals that continuously conveyed that he was fully engaged with Dan. He listened keenly; His questions, wherever he wanted clarification, were short, sharp, and pertinent.

"I have always thought that you and I have similar operating styles. This was further reinforced by the recent self-awareness that I have acquired through my new knowledge and learnings." Dan paused briefly, "I am not sure if you agree with my assessment, but I firmly believe that these will help you as much as they have helped me in the past few weeks."

As Dan finished speaking, he handed Tom the summary of learning that he had completed last night at home.

Dan's Learnings
Ron's Success Mantras?

1. **VALUE people and empower them to peak performance.**

2. **THINK first, watch NONVERBALS; ASK to learn, LISTEN to understand.**

3. **Clarify the INTENT before any conversation to avoid misinterpretation.**

4. **Forego CONTROL to build and strengthen relationships.**

5. **Care for people selflessly to induce INFLUENCE and COMMITMENT.**

6. **Use every CONFLICT as an opportunity to ENGAGE.**

"I have summarized my learnings in these six points. I suggest that you reflect on what I shared today, review this summary and then we meet again in a few days. What do you think?"

"I can't thank you enough, Dan. The past two hours have been the most valuable and have given me excellent insights. I now need to internalize them." He paused, hesitated as he chose his words carefully, "This should not surprise you when I say that I hold you in extremely high esteem. I had never thought that we both have similar operating styles as I have not really been aware of mine. But as you were talking today, I could see shades of me in many areas."

"In the past few weeks, we have all noticed huge change in you, for the better. Everyone feels positive about it. Now that I know the cause, your learnings have become even more meaningful and valuable for me."

"Excellent" Dan said. "I am glad you have noticed the change. I am confident that you too can make similar positive change. Let's meet next week at the same time. Thanks for your time, Tom."

They got up, shook hands, and walked out of the huddle room.

As Tom walked away, Dan wandered into his thought-land. *'Opening to someone, more so your subordinate, and sharing your vulnerabilities is harder than I had thought. At times it became so tough that I almost chocked.'* A shiver went down his spine as he relived that moment. *'But it was well worth it; I think I strengthened my relationship with Tom today. Going by his nonverbals, I made a significant impact on him. Selfless care for the people does work. Great experience. I will certainly do more of it.'*

As he was about to reach his desk, another thought struck like lightening. He had to sit down. *'Haven't I discovered something? A lose-win surrender can also lead to win-win engagement! That is what really happened with Tom. My surrender melted his anxiousness and made him comfortable to engage effectively. There are probably many ways to reach the engagement point; it is situational! I must capture this.'*

He pulled out his laptop and started typing.

As he finished, Anita was waiting for him. The day at The Global Company had just begun.

The week was progressing well for Dan until the monthly review meeting of his leadership team on Friday morning. Tom got into a verbal duel with one of his peers, Rob O'Brian, who had questioned an approach Tom was proposing; it was the same old Tom after that! Being irrational at times but mostly operating from a control space trying to dominate and go for win-lose. Dan was deeply disappointed at Tom's behavior, which showed almost no signs of any learnings from their discussion on Monday.

Dan decided against intervening. He had no desire to take sides and wanted to give Tom a full opportunity to use his learnings to manage a situation like this. While they continued their tiff, Dan went to his thought-land.

'It does not look like Tom took anything out of our discussion. He missed all important lessons on effective communication, influencing and conflict management. He looked so engaged and eager to practice his new learnings when we were discussing. What has happened? He was looking good until Rob asked that question. And then all was lost. Why?'

Dan had to intervene ten minutes later as Tom and Rob were still at it.

"Guys, I suggest that you two take it offline and engage me if required, but I want you to resolve this conflict by yourselves. Can I expect that?" Dan asked and continued when they both nodded.

"As we have already covered all agenda topics and still have some time available, I want to share with you an important concept – conflict management. We may probably overshoot our original scheduled time by thirty minutes; is everyone okay with that?" They all nodded.

Dan chose to talk conflict management deliberately. There were several reasons. First, apart from the behavior of Tom and Rob in the meeting, he believed that his team lacked this skill, including him! Second, he figured that as conflict management requires almost all his new skills, this will be a great way to share his learnings with the team. Third, he knew that the best way to learn is by teaching.

He connected his laptop and projected the conflict square on the screen.

While staying on the broader subject of conflict management, Dan highlighted the gist of his learnings of the past few weeks. One hour later he concluded, "Conflicts are natural because we are diverse individuals; there will always be different points of views. The real challenge is to stay open and either influence or be influenced or agree to disagree. Finding ways to a win-win solution is critical for not only our relationships but also our results."

"I will be glad to take questions now?"

Everyone enjoyed the training; they could relate to Dan's discourse and to his changed behavior and actions. They were all pleased with new Dan.

"Thanks, Dan. This is quite helpful. My question is how we should handle people who are not open to either being influenced or agree to disagree. In other words, who believe that theirs is the only possible approach." It was Rob asking in obvious reference to Tom and the argument they just had.

Dan practiced ThERe before answering in a measured tone, "Excellent question, Rob. A conflict happens when our wants are mutually impossible. Often, debate or argument starts, as it happened earlier today, even before exploring the potential commonality of the needs. And almost always we think and blame the other for being irrational and the cause of the conflict." He paused, looking at Rob.

"The other person certainly has a role, but we too share it equally. Both hands are required to clap! Most often our ego-act neglects empathy."

He paused again for the impact. "If we can understand and appreciate that an external conflict cannot grow unless 'both' parties are involved, and I too have an equal role; many conflicts can be avoided."

"If you and Tom are game, we can do an assessment of how your earlier conflict could have been avoided."

"What do you guys say? Will it be a valuable learning opportunity?" He asked the team. They all said yes in unison, except Tom and Rob who were hesitant initially but finally nodded looking at the response of others.

Tom took the first shot rather emotionally, "I realize that I took Rob's challenge to my proposal personally and reacted to it somewhat insensitively." He stopped briefly and continued after he was able to control his emotions, "Being transparent, what threw me off was the feeling that Rob asked the question not to seek information but to pull me and my proposal down. I somehow lost my objectivity, and after that it was all about defending myself." It was Tom's attempt at engaging Rob.

Rob, who was listening to Tom intently, immediately responded, "Thanks for your transparency, Tom. I really appreciate it. I too must admit that my reactions were also uncalled for. Although I had no intent to pull you down, I probably framed my question negatively. In fact, I like your proposal; it will improve productivity on many of my production lines. I plan to invite you so that we can review and discuss the detail in my leadership team meeting."

Tom's face lit up. He instantly got up, shook Rob's hands, and replied with a huge smile, "Any time, Rob. It will be my pleasure."

Everyone was watching this fascinating transformation and live demonstration of what Dan had just taught them. Dan could not have asked for anything better.

With a smile he addressed his team, "What you just witnessed is an exceptional example of engagement in win-win flow manner after demotivating lose-lose friction just one hour back. Tom engaged Rob with empathy and transparently explained the reasons for losing it. And Rob immediately responded with similar transparency and empathy. "It is great that the conflict has been resolved in win-win flow! But could the earlier friction have been avoided?" he asked.

It was Paula who replied, "Yes. I think it could have been if Rob had prefaced his question with what he explained later. I will use Rob's words but paraphrase them for better understanding." She paused and continued, '*I really like your proposal, Tom. It has the potential to improve productivity on many of my production lines. I plan to invite you to my leadership team meeting so that we can review it with my team. However, I need a clarification....,*' the discussion one hour back would have been different and positive."

"Excellent, Paula. Questions or 'ask' is a critical part of communication. Most of us do not realize the power and associated risks of 'ask'. Let me give you a simple example.

Many years back, one of my older team members, who was rather tardy and curt in responding to my questions, provided me with an incredible insight. He said and I quote, *'Please do not begin your questions with a 'why...'; I find it intimidating and somewhat insulting. Instead, if you use 'Please help me understand...,' I will be inspired to genuinely help you understand.'* Unquote. I have always followed that suggestion."

They exchanged glances and smiled as they now knew why Dan's questions always began with 'Please help me understand...'

Oblivious to their smiles, Dan continued, "Effective communication is **not only what to say** but even more importantly about **how to say it** and **what not to say**." He paused and made eye contact with almost all of them. "Nothing could have explained it better than what we just witnessed."

"If there are no other questions or comments, let us quickly review the summary of our agreements and action steps." The meeting was adjourned fifteen minutes later.

Dan was immensely pleased with himself and how he conducted the meeting and the training. More importantly, he was extremely excited about how the conflict was resolved. In a way he wanted to thank Tom for creating a learning opportunity for all, but it was quite concerning too; he was undecided whether Tom's action was justified notwithstanding his later explanation.

'Did Rob really give him a reason to lose it? I am not sure. I must assess in detail.' Despite the learning opportunity, the event had discolored an otherwise cheerful day. In that somber mood he walked into the cafeteria for lunch.

THIRTEEN

Dan stopped at Linda's desk on his way to Ron's next session. "How are you doing today?" he asked with a bright smile. Linda responded with a joyful smile and wave of hand. "He is waiting for you," is all she said.

Ron was on his feet as soon as he saw Dan. They exchanged pleasantries and settled down on the corner sofa where Dan's steaming Starbucks coffee waited.

"How was the week, Dan? I am very eager to hear your learnings." Ron asked.

"I had a good week. My biggest learning was that lose-win surrender is a step towards win-win engagement." Dan had decided he would not share anything about the morning event.

Ron had to control his eyebrows. "You always bring a new learning for me, Dan." He said with a smile. "Cannot wait to hear it. Please describe the situation so that I can understand. And please withhold the names as they will not add any value."

Excitedly, Dan narrated his Monday discussion with Tom and how his lose-win surrender had allowed Tom to calm down and open. Tom's name was not used.

"Interesting," is all Ron said. He was quiet for few minutes before he asked, "Dan, why do you think it was surrender?"

"I apologized several times. I was honest and exposed my vulnerability to a subordinate. It clearly was 'surrender' Ron."

"Dan, what makes you think that an apology was needed? Had you harmed this person? Did you do anything with ill intent?"

Dan was taken aback by the line of Ron's questions. So, he thought carefully before replying, "No, Ron, I had neither harmed nor did anything with ill intent." He paused and took a deep breath before continuing, "But it so happened that this person misinterpreted my words and my motive as I did not describe my intent due to my own insecurity."

Ron became aware of Dan's discomfort with this conversation, but he had no choice. It had to be taken to its logical conclusion.

"It must have been a combination of retrospection, assessment and introspection that helped you realize that you must apologize and honestly share your insecurities to re-engage this person. It must have been very tough."

He did not wait for Dan's response and continued, "My intent is not to make you uncomfortable Dan but to help you understand a very important aspect of what we have learned in the past few weeks."

Dan was quiet and visibly anxious as Ron continued.

"You did not surrender, Dan; you engaged. You did it because of your compassion for this person. Because, neither in control nor in empathy you would have gone that far to expose your insecurity or vulnerability. You were operating with selfless care and concern for this individual. And in return you must have got complete commitment to whatever you were asking. Am I interpreting it correctly, Dan?"

Dan was speechless as a tsunami of emotions flooded him. Ron had compassionately taken the wind off the sails of his 'brilliant' discovery. When he finally found his voice, it was soft and feeble, "Thanks, Ron. What I thought was profound learning just turned upside down! I can see it clearly now; it was not surrender. Instead, I slowly and surely converted the previous win-lose to a win-win. I successfully engaged and gained this person's full commitment." A smile finally sneaked in as he completed the sentence.

"Dan, your interpretation may have been different, but your handling of the conflict is impressive and praiseworthy. It is very tough to internalize learnings so fast."

"I may want to take credit for it as your teacher, but it will be foolhardy! Teaching is the easy part; the difficult part is for the individual to consistently practice new behaviors. It makes me proud to see you do it so well. It will be great learning for me if you can describe how you have achieved it."

Dan was flushed with such expansive praise from his role model. He chose his words thoughtfully, "Ron, even I am surprised. I have had numerous trainings in my nineteen years with The Global Company. The 'training euphoria' remained for a few days and then, phew it vanished. It is different this time; short-term instant elation of new learning has been replaced by gradual awareness of wisdom. I am using big words, Ron, but this is exactly how I feel." He paused to take a deep breath. "I have spent considerable time thinking about the reasons for such a change. I could identify three."

"First, quest for knowledge brought me to you, and I found a guru."

"A small digression may help explain what I mean. In ancient India, teaching was a highly respected profession and teachers were categorized; guru being the most revered. Although we use these words interchangeably, the Indians differentiate guru from teacher very succinctly, and I quote, *'The teacher gives us knowledge while the guru gives us wisdom, the teacher answers our questions while the guru questions our answers, the teacher sharpens our mind while the guru opens our mind, the teacher takes responsibility for our growth while the guru makes us responsible for our growth.'"*

"You have become my guru." Deep gratitude and respect were clearly audible and visible in Dan's voice and eyes.

Ron sat fascinated and his face showed it.

"Second, your compassion drove my commitment. I am determined to learn and apply as I cannot let down my guru and his huge investment in me."

"Third, you made learning simple by distilling knowledge into focused segments and easy to understand concepts. This gave me the opportunity to seek, soak and sift, and take baby steps in reapplication. Early wins became the inspiration for more and more reapplication. Now, in every situation I think, how can I use my learnings here?"

"Dan, you put me on a pedestal that I don't deserve. The credit is totally yours as I explained earlier. But I love your description of guru versus teacher. Yes, we in the West use the word guru rather arbitrarily. You would recall that while discussing communication, we said that people use English words differently based on their cultural background. This is a great example. I will be careful in my use of the word guru from here on."

"More importantly, Dan, you have unknowingly created a model for learning. I am not sure if you got all your answers, but you have certainly given me answers to the questions that I did not even have." He laughed.

Dan liked what he heard but was puzzled; he had no clue of the model he just created! He thought communicating through 'silence' was wiser than exhibiting ignorance."

"What do you think, Dan? Have your questions been answered?"

Dan found his voice. "More than answered. I feel blessed that I came to you. The past few weeks have transformed my personal and work life. I cannot thank you enough."

"No need to thanks me. It is all because of your commitment. Seek, Soak, and Sift, using your words, which I very much like. But to complete the model, allow me the liberty to add another S – Share.

Dan was elated and thought to himself, *'Did not realize that my wordplay was a model!'* Pleased with his decision to keep his ignorance to himself, he asked intelligently, "I am not clear about share, Ron? The other three 'S' words— Seek, Soak and Sift— are all internal to me. Share is external."

"Great question. You were able to put your newly acquired knowledge into practice because you converted it into learnings by 'sharing' it with yourself. This sharing brings a commitment and restlessness to convert the knowledge into practice."

"The euphoria of training is not sustained because we compartmentalize and lock new knowledge into our 'reference library' for future use."

"Our learning is complete only when we share the knowledge or make it available to ourselves for day-to-day use. You did it. So, the four 'S' words of learning are Seek, Soak, Sift and Share. They are the true reason for this transformation in your life."

"Another model! You are fast becoming the 'model man' Dan," he laughed.

Dan did not know where to look. He just smiled, walked up to the white board, drew a picture, and looked at Ron. "What do you think?"

Ron came up, studied the picture for some time, then made a few changes.

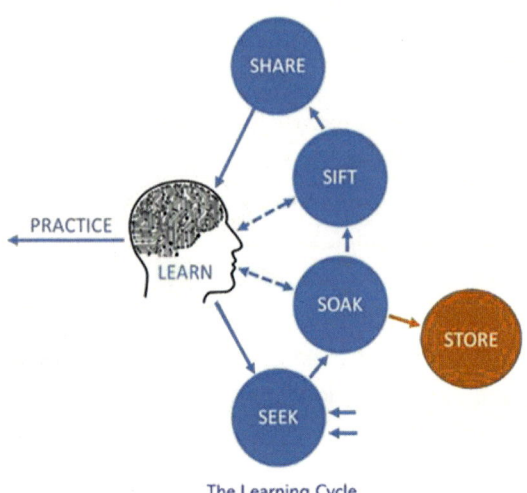

The Learning Cycle

"There is another 'S' word that we want to avoid – Store. Knowledge, once stored, is no longer available for sharing, and learning stops."

"It can also go in store if the 'Seek' is weak, i.e., when we find that the knowledge, being forced on us through institutional or organizational training, is either not relevant or not new. Weak 'seek' automatically results in weak 'soak' that does not create enough momentum to take it to 'sift' and 'share'; instead, it moves to 'store.' Learning stops!"

"I am still somewhat confused, Ron. I thought I had got it but now I am not so sure. When I acquire knowledge, am I not learning?"

"I am glad you are still seeking," Ron replied smiling. "Knowledge remains knowledge till we practice and use it. We can practice only when knowledge is available to us through our sharing." He paused.

"Sharing within ourselves is the process of understanding and assimilating the knowledge that transforms it into learning. Practice can start only when it becomes our learning. And that is when knowledge turns into wisdom," Ron concluded.

"Our model now has five 'S' words. Unfortunately, we cannot call it that because '5S' already exists – The Japanese workplace organization method. So, what should we call our model? How about **The Learning Cycle**?" Ron glanced at Dan inquisitively.

"Sounds good. It is now clear. You are right. I spent hours understanding and assimilating what you taught me. I was able to practice these concepts only after that. It would otherwise have been very superficial and inconsistent."

"Thanks for taking time to explain this. The addition of 'share' and 'store' and your explanation has innovated my 'wordplay' into a powerful concept. As I think of it, this was the real issue with my earlier failed trainings and the reason for my recent successes."

"It is also consistent with the framework of learn-do-teach. Although, teach cannot happen unless people trust you."

"Thank you for this segue into another critically important topic, Dan – Trust." Ron laughed again. "What is it?"

"Firm belief in ability, reliability and integrity of someone or something," Dan replied without second thought.

"True. This is what the dictionary will say. Let me ask you differently. Do you trust me? If yes, why?"

Dan had to think because the question had now become personal and required a choice of right words. "I trust you because I have a firm belief that you will not do anything that may harm me in any way. And that you will always be honest with me."

"Is there a contradiction in what you say, Dan? What if my honest communication or feedback hurts your feelings?"

Dan had no answer.

Ron continued, "It is true that consistently honest and transparent communications and dealings build trust. However, honesty and transparency are neither saying things that can hurt nor are they saying incorrect and insincere things that flatter." He paused for a moment, "Recall we talked, 'effective communication is not only what to say, but also what not to say.' Words that can hurt are better unspoken. Honest feedback is essential, but it must be provided in a way that is neither hurtful nor compromises the message. Prefacing the message with clear intent provides the right context and helps."

Dan was reminded of his first botched-up meeting with Tom.

Ron continued, "The notion that 'it is difficult to give honest feedback to people' is both true and false. Without trust, it is extremely difficult because it could lead to misinterpretation, misunderstanding and conflict. On the other hand, it can build trust if the intent is sincere, selfless and without an ulterior motive, and the feedback is clearly articulated in a positive and constructive way that inspires."

"Let me now ask you another question. Do you think I trust you, Dan?"

"I think you do. Otherwise, it might be difficult for me to trust you."

"Exactly. Trust begets trust; you will not be able to trust me if I do not trust you. Similarly, mutual respect is an important prerequisite for trust. It is almost impossible for trust to build without respect for the individual."

"That is true. But for gaining my trust, people must earn it."

"Well said, Dan. We trust only those who have reliably and consistently demonstrated their trustworthiness, not only to us but also to others. This last part is very crucial."

"Would you trust a person who is consistent and honest with

you but may behave in an unscrupulous way with others?

"I would have a problem trusting such a person as he could do the same with me in future. Integrity plays an important role in trusting someone," Dan replied.

"What do you mean by integrity, Dan?"

"To me, it means being honest, truthful, principled," Dan said.

Ron nodded in affirmative. "Integrity, though the cornerstone of trust, can be interpreted in many ways in this context. For example, even the most virtuous person may be considered less trustworthy by me compared to a person who lies to protect me!"

"Integrity is often a bond between two individuals or entities, and they choose to interpret it in their own preferred way."

"Sometimes 'unconditional-allegiance-come-what-may' is considered integrity. This unquestioned loyalty, specific to an individual or an institution, can be induced either through materialistic enticement out of greed or through control out of fear or through compassion out of deep reverence. Unfortunately, in either case it is superficial and unsustainable, and has a higher chance of ending up in betrayal."

"When we trust someone, we have a firm belief that they will never betray the faith we have entrusted in them. Sustainable trust is a relationship built on mutual respect, understanding, and confidence of consistency, dependability, and predictability. Although there is no expectation for the other to agree and endorse everything we say or do, their behavior and actions are expected to be rational and within the guidelines of agreed principles."

"Ron does this mean that we must define and align to a set

of principles in every relationship?" Dan enquired.

"Ideally, yes, though almost all relationships already have some inherent principles. For example, fidelity is a critical principle in a marriage just as meeting commitments is essential in a work relationship."

"It helps immensely to align the principles of a relationship with our partners to insure it against misunderstanding and misinterpretation." Ron paused.

"Do you remember '**Expectations Swap**', the exercise we conducted when I came back as the director. We were aligning the principles of our relationship."

Dan went back to the time when Ron had returned to their department as their boss and the first thing he did was to ask all his direct reports, that included Dan, to conduct an exercise that he called 'Expectations Swap'. Each one of them was asked to write three to four points under two headings:

- What I expect from Ron
- What I think Ron expects from me

Ron did the same for each one of them and reviewed both the documents one-on-one with each team member. The purpose was to clarify, understand and align mutual expectations.

"I recall it vividly, Ron. We thought it to be the 'new' thing of the new boss. But it really helped as we became clear about what you expected from us, and we were confident that you too understood what we expected from you. It proved to be quite helpful as our behavior and actions were then guided by these expectations."

"I am glad you found it useful. The most common reason for breach of trust is unknown or guessed expectations. What we presume is acceptable, surprises the other person as our actions or words do not meet their expectations. Unfortunately, most often the expectations are neither defined nor aligned, resulting in perceived breach of trust! And as trust is the foundation, it affects the relationship. Trust, in early stages of a relationship, is so fragile that even a perceived breach can break it."

"Trust, they say takes a long time to build, seconds to break and forever to repair."

"Ron, this is a very important subject. I am wondering how we can manage trust and expectations in a relationship.

"It is an excellent but extraordinarily complex question, Dan. The answer too is quite difficult. Because a cookie cutter approach is not possible." He paused for a few moments. For the first time Dan had a feeling that Ron was grappling for words.

After a while Ron spoke, "I have never thought about this before. As you have again brought me to unchartered territory, you will have to bear with me; we will jointly try to find the answer." He was silent again, deep in thought.

"Relationships are all about trust and expectations. It is impractical to define a common set of expectations or principles for all relationships as diversity of the individuals makes every relationship distinct and unique." He paused again; eyes focused on the ceiling.

"The only way to sustain and strengthen a relationship is to manage the expectations of the partner effectively."

"Expectations swap, that we talked about earlier, is an excellent tool for work relationships where expectations are straightforward and knowing them is sufficient to manage the relationship."

"In personal relationship the expectations are layered and far more complex. They are the fickle version of the 'wants' of conflict management with wings of fantasy. They are unpredictable, can change rapidly and are not dependent on pragmatism. They are more like 'wishes' that can overwhelm us if not managed effectively."

"Such expectations have stages that I will try to capture in a picture." He walked to the whiteboard and started to draw.

While Ron was drawing, Dan was wandering into thought-land, *'How can Ron do this? Although this complex subject is new and made him uncomfortable in the beginning, he is now explaining it like the master who knows it inside out. I will ask him at an appropriate time.'*

Ron was finally satisfied after several iterations. He then asked Dan to join him at the board.

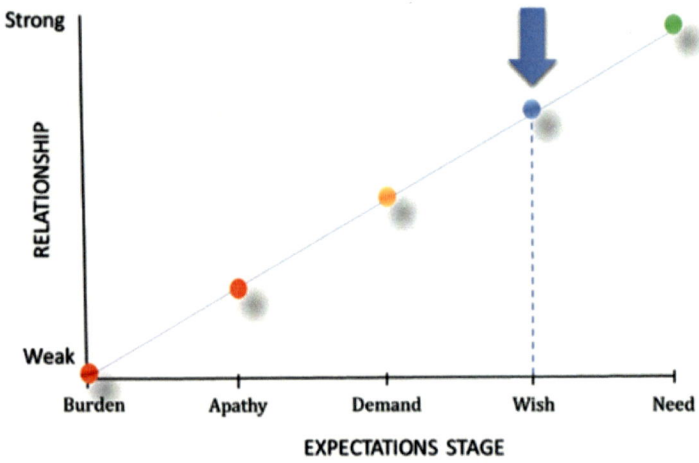

"Probably best to call it '**The Expectations Conundrum**' – the challenges of expectations." He said, pointing at what he had drawn. "The continuum of expectations in a personal relationship is quite diverse. In most relationships, the expectations start as 'wish,' the dotted vertical line with the arrow. Relationship can go in any direction from there! Either slide down or get stronger."

"Unmanaged, 'wish' can become 'demand' that is one-sided, rigid, inflexible, and difficult to meet. Invariably, it will slowly drift towards 'apathy,' where partners take each other for granted because they lose enthusiasm and are neither concerned nor care. It can slide further to the worst stage, 'burden' where expectations become responsibility, and the relationship becomes a deadweight, steadily moving towards the breakpoint." He paused.

"Every 'wish' is the face of some invisible and unmet 'need.' If the partners can maturely identify and understand that need, they can significantly enhance the chances of meeting it and strengthen the relationship."

His relationship with Betsy suddenly flashed through Dan's mind which, he was sure, had almost reached 'apathy.' *'Thanks to you, Ron, I was able to rescue our relationship. This is fantastic learning. I must understand it better.'* He thought.

"How do you think we can ensure that wishes do not drift towards demand, Dan?" Ron asked, now in complete command.

"It should be similar to conflict management, I guess; we have to engage our partner to identify the need behind the wish and look for commonality," Dan replied.

"Yes, while the basics are the same, there is some difference in expectations management. There are three steps. First, define and align the needs of your relationship, jointly and transparently. Second, convert these expectations into a set of principles that guide the behaviors and actions of both partners. Third, strictly follow these aligned principles."

"Otherwise, the relationship, however old and strong, will always remain susceptible to the risks of misunderstanding and misinterpretation.

"This is a fantastic concept, Ron. Enormously powerful and

extremely easy to understand. It clearly explains how relations can be strengthened by proper management of expectations. I am wondering, however, are there any relationships without expectations?"

"Great question but you got me again, Dan. I will have to think this through." Ron paused, deep in thought. He started hesitatingly.

"I believe all relationships come with their own different and unique expectations. The only relationship without expectations, that I can think of, is true friendship. This is off-the-cuff so you may want to 'sift' this; I believe that life-long friendship can only develop when friends do not expect anything from each other." He paused again to think.

"Chemistry or like-mindedness can create the desire to be friends, but a lasting friendship is only possible when the relationship is devoid of expectations. Does it make sense?"

"It does somewhat but there is a question, Ron. Materialistic expectations may be absent in a true friendship, but emotional expectations do exist. I would certainly look up to my friends for emotional and moral support in time of crisis."

By now Ron was the master again, "Great point. An expectation is a 'desire to receive' something either in return of something we do or because of our relationship like parent-child, husband-wife, siblings etc. It is almost like a right."

"True friendship, on the other hand, is not about receiving but giving. That is why I consider it to be the highest form of relationship. True friends have the commitment and confidence that they will always be there for each other. This is not an expectation but a conviction. What form or shape 'we-will-always-be-there-for-us' takes is unknown because it is not an expectation. What we give will be based on the need depending on the situation. It could be mere presence for emotional and moral support or even material support. True friends neither know nor bother to find out beforehand. Their conviction in each other is complete and is devoid of any expectations."

"It may sound like semantics, but it is not. Every expectation has a defined shape and parameter. My trust and conviction in my true friends are abstract, formless and cannot be defined."

"Is it clearer or did I confuse you further?" asked Ron.

"Thanks. I got it. Where will you place true friendship in the conundrum of expectations?"

Ron smiled, "I don't think it belongs there. Do you have a different thought, Dan?"

Dan was quietly looking at Ron's model. He walked to the whiteboard, looked at Ron and asked, "May I?" Without waiting for a response, he started editing the model as Ron watched him in fascination.

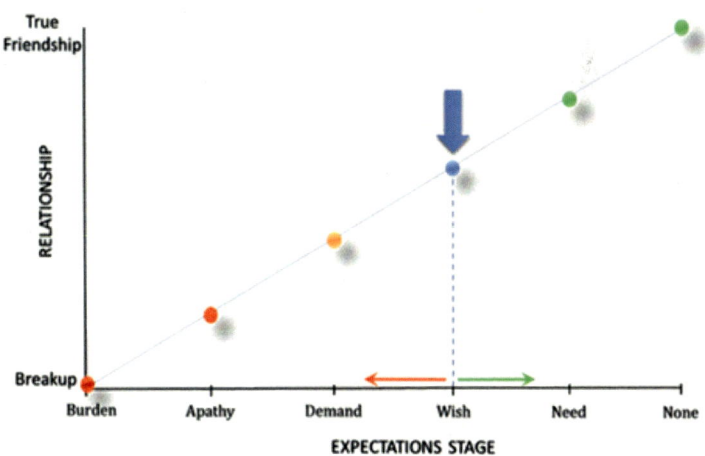

Expectations Conundrum

"Wow. This is fantastic! You have made the model far more powerful now. I was not totally satisfied with it as I knew something was missing but I could not comprehend. It is now complete. Thanks."

"I do not deserve thanks. I just transcribed your words into your picture. I was amazed when you created this outstanding model within minutes; it sums up the challenges of relationships so beautifully in an easy-to-understand picture. To me it was a live display of 'think first' and your clarity of thought."

Ron just smiled his happy smile.

Dan continued, "Today was an enormously powerful lesson on an extremely critical subject that puts many things in perspective. Though a new topic for you, the simplicity of your explanation has directly taken it to sift for me."

"You have shared several concepts in the past few weeks that have answered far more than the question that brought me to you. They are even more powerful for me because I see a role model in you who embodies them. This is what really inspired me to try to learn and practice."

"In summary, I now well understand these concepts but am still struggling somewhat as to how do they all fit together?"

Ron laughed loudly, "Excellent question as usual. That is what we will discuss in the next sessions. I suggest you think about it until we meet again. If there are no other questions, let us call it a day."

"Thanks, Ron. I have no other questions, for now."

They wished each other goodbye and shook hands. "Have a great weekend, Dan," Ron said as Dan walked out.

On the way home, Dan's thoughts moved to Tom, and he wondered about the morning incident.

'Did I waste my time with him on Monday? Why did he not

follow the concepts we had discussed?'

'He had strong 'seek.' I am sure of that. Going by his body language and the questions, even 'soak' was strong. The slip may have come in 'sift' and certainly he did not 'share.' How can I ensure that he learns? I will need to spend time to think this out over the weekend.'

'I also need to think about expectations swap. It is really a powerful method. I must try it with Tom. Probably it is time to do it with Betsy as well. Although with Betsy it has to be more than expectations swap – we have to understand each other's needs. Can it be possible to transform our relationship to true friendship?'

'I think it is time to share the details of my learnings with Betsy. I must not delay it any further. She will be excited to know what has pulled our relationship from the brink and where we can take it from here.'

As he entered the driveway, he saw Betsy talking to their neighbor Anne Chopra. They both waved at him. He stopped the car and joined them.

The weekend had begun.

FOURTEEN

Betsy and Dan spent a lively evening at Chopra home, celebrating Anne's birthday. Wine flowed as the evening passed and the party got noisier. Amid all the fun and frolic Dan noticed that Karan and Anne were not their usual self. In fact, they seemed to be acting as a 'happy couple' with abysmal results. This deeply concerned him as the Chopras were not only their neighbors and good friends but also a lovely couple.

Getting home past midnight, Dan brought up the subject with Betsy, "Did you notice something unusual at the party, Bet?"

"Anne shared a few things with me earlier in the evening. I wanted to tell you but did not get a chance in the rush to go to their party. Yes, not everything is fine. As we both care for them, it will be a long discussion, Dan. Let's talk about it tomorrow."

"Sure. Can we talk at the golf course, or should we cancel our game tomorrow?"

"It will be much better if we do it uninterrupted. Discussing at home will be much better,"

Dan nodded, pulled out his mobile, opened the golf club app and canceled their booking.

They were both up early the next day as the night was rather restless. After a quick breakfast, they sat in the garden. Neither of them had said anything about the Chopras this morning.

"Anne came over yesterday evening an hour before you returned from work. On the face of it she came to remind me of her birthday party, but I think she wanted to discuss Karan and her situation. She looked disturbed as she felt that their relationship is going downhill. She told me that Karan and She don't seem to care about each other anymore; it is very frustrating for her as she still loves him and thinks that he does too. She does not know why this is happening.

Dan was listening attentively. He spoke only after he was sure Betsy had finished.

"Bet, before we discuss the Chopras, I want to talk about us." Seeing the anxiousness that suddenly appeared on Betsy's face, he held her hand and continued without taking a breath, "We have not discussed this, but we know that our relationship has transformed, for the better." He smiled as Betsy's trademark lovely smile replaced the anxiety.

"For a moment you frightened me, Dan Webber." She chuckled. "The past few weeks have been remarkable. Despite huge curiosity about the cause of this change, I have been hesitant to bring it up for fear of breaking this enviable spell."

Dan leaned over, hugged Betsy and whispered in her ear, "This spell will never break, Bet. If anything, you and I will make it stronger and longer."

She held him tightly and they stayed that way until Dan spoke again. "I want to share with you what has changed."

Betsy sat there spellbound, motionless, as Dan narrated the whole story about his frustration at work, seeking Ron's help, his learnings, and his attempt to bring those learnings into practice. He explained how things had dramatically changed at work since then. He looked Betsy directly in the eyes and added with a sly smile, "And at home."

Betsy responded with an even bigger smile. "Dan, this is so beautiful and romantic. But I feel devastated that you had to endure so much pressure and anguish at work and I could not share it; I should have tried to find out. You poor darling!" and she hugged him. "Thanks for getting us back." She whispered.

"It is not just me, Bet. You played an equally important role. We could never be here without your positive response. Without your enthusiastic reciprocity, I would have gone back into my shell after a few tries. Your response encouraged and inspired me."

"I don't know how many times I thought of taking the initiative myself, but I was so afraid that you may not respond. Not sure whether the fear of rejection was too strong or was it my ego that prevented me from taking the lead. But I was clear that I would grab it with both hands if you ever initiated. Every time we were nearby or talked, I hoped and waited!"

"I was in the same boat. My ego and loss-of-face fear were not allowing me to initiate. Although I too had created numerous mental scenarios of how I would respond if ever you reached out. I too hoped and waited every day!"

"Then in the very first session with Ron I learned the value of valuing people. I also realized that I value you and our relationship far more than my ego."

"I had no idea how you would respond, but that became irrelevant. I was prepared for the worst, and I would have been distraught if you had responded negatively, but I would feel satisfied that at least I tried. Thank goodness, for your response that pleasantly surprised me." He smiled holding her hand tightly.

"Although hoping and waiting for you to initiate, I too was surprised at the suddenness of your first approach and was unsure whether it was real, deliberate and how long it would last. But I wanted to play along as I was extremely unhappy where we were.

Lo and behold, it not only lasted but kept getting better by the day!" She was looking fondly at Dan.

Instinctively, it was the most appropriate moment for a long passionate kiss. After regaining their breath, they just sat there holding each other, smiling.

Dan gently moved, picking up the papers he had brought with him.

"Bet, I had already decided to share this with you today. Chopras' situation makes it even more relevant."

He shared Dan's Triangle of Relationships and his theory of control space, and why he believed it to be the root cause of their drift. He also explained that the transformation in their relationship had been caused by their move up to empathy and compassion space. Betsy murmured, "This is fascinating and so true."

Dan then shared the Expectations Conundrum. Betsy looked at it speechless.

"Bet, where do you think we were on the expectations spectrum a few weeks back?"

"Somewhere between demand and apathy, closer to apathy I would think. Although we both wanted to mend, we were unwilling to take the first step and the outward enthusiasm towards each other had started to wane. Our expectations had already become inflexible and our demands uncompromising."

"You are right. I feel the same. Now we are somewhere between wish and need. Our strong desire for a healthy relationship and unwillingness to upset the applecart has kept our wishes in check. But this is not sustainable. We will have to understand the needs that are driving our wishes. Then only can we look for synergies and understand and align our mutual needs. It will enhance trust and further strengthen our relationship."

"I am delighted that we can discuss such a sensitive subject so transparently, openly sharing our feelings and vulnerabilities. Don't you think it displays the robustness and maturity of our relationship, Dan? Do we still need to align our expectation needs?"

"Yes, I do. This alignment is essential to add the critical third adjective to our relationship – long lasting or sustainable. None of us would like to go back to where we were a few weeks back – we need robust, mature, and sustainable relationship."

"It could probably also put us on the path to 'No Expectations' and true friendship."

"That will be outstanding. I am keen to work towards that. I will have to think about it some more, but an expectation-free life-long lovely friendship with you seems quite intriguing." She gave him a huge smile and winked.

"Where do the Chopras fit in this?" asked Betsy.

"I think they may be where we were a few weeks back."

"Then, they also can pull back like us as they too are very fond of each other. Right?"

"Yes, but it will all depend on the strength of their desire to mend things. My bigger fear, however, is that we are not relationship counselors and could complicate things further."

"But we cannot leave it without trying either; this is the friendship *dharma*. If nothing else, we can probably become the icebreaker that we had so desperately yearned for in our relationship. Most likely they too are hoping and waiting."

"What if we invite them for a golf game tomorrow? That will give us several hours to talk to both individually. Over lunch we can do the collective thing." Betsy asked and looked at Dan inquisitively.

"Brilliant idea." Dan lit up. "Let me call Karan and you do

the same with Anne. How about 7:00 a.m. tee-off?"

"Let me call Anne right away. You make the booking at the club." Betsy and Dan picked up their phones almost simultaneously.

The next morning, Betsy and Dan were up early for the golf game. Anne and Karan had accepted their invitation without much hesitation. Perhaps they too were looking for a facilitator or maybe they wanted to avoid being alone together.

They were waiting when Dan parked his car at the club. After pleasantries, they registered and walked to the changing rooms together.

The starter guided them to Hole Number One which had an eight-minute wait. They drew partners – Betsy-Anne and Dan-Karan. Betsy and Dan could not have asked for a better draw as it would give both a chance to discuss the issue openly.

So, it was girls vs boys. They agreed to four-ball play and aligned the handicaps.

Betsy and Anne combined well. Betsy and Dan did most of the talking; Anne and Karan were quiet and distant. Their answers were monosyllables.

Dan was unable to have a meaningful conversation as Karan was too cautious and chose to respond to Dan's questions rather ambiguously.

'How can I draw him out? It will have to be done very sensitively.'

As they finished back nine, the girls were up two holes. There was no celebration.

They showered, changed, and joined in the bar. Dan started the conversation once they had ordered their drinks and snacks.

"Betsy and I feel really privileged to have you both as our neighbors and friends. We have known each other for several years. It is apparent that all is not well with you two. But we respect you and your privacy and are confident that you will make us part of it whenever you are ready to share. We invited you today because we want to share our story and what has happened to us over the past few weeks."

He paused and looked at Anne and Karan who seemed disinterested and were avoiding his eye contact.

"We do not know exactly when Betsy and I started to drift apart. We do not know what caused it but were both aware that something was wrong. We also did not know what to do despite being unhappy about it."

"Few weeks back I started to consult a colleague about some work situation. That gave me several learnings which I thought could be applied even in our personal life. I started to practice those learnings at home and Betsy responded very positively. The most important thing, that we later learned, is that both of us were waiting for the other to initiate the first step," Dan said.

The body language of both had changed and Anne and Karan were listening to Dan with interest.

'It is a good sign.' Dan thought, reading the nonverbals, and continued.

"In a few weeks since then, we have stopped the drift and transformed our relationship. To be honest, we were this close only during the early years."

"I don't want to impose, but if you feel comfortable, I can share a few important learnings."

Karan and Anne exchanged a quick glance with each other and nodded.

He shared the Expectations Conundrum and explained it to them.

"Every personal relationship has a set of unique expectations between the partners. These expectations start as wishes, emanating from some basic needs. If these needs are not met fully, wishes begin to grow exponentially and harden into demand, which is more rigid and inflexible. It leads to apathy where the partners begin to lose enthusiasm towards each other. Next, the expectations become burden and so does the relationship."

"On the other side, relationships can be strengthened when the partners identify and understand the needs that are driving their wishes. Convert the aligned needs into principles to guide their everyday behavior and actions. The ultimate bliss can be achieved if the relationship becomes expectation-free."

"Betsy and I were close to apathy a few weeks back. Turning it back has been an exhilarating journey since. We still have to understand and align the exact needs of our relationship to make it sustainable, but we have certainly pulled back from the brink. Still an exceedingly long way to even know if we can ever get to the world of expectation-free relationship."

By now, Anne and Karan were eagerly soaking every word out of Dan's mouth and were no longer as anxious as when the conversation started. But they were still pensive, quiet, and looked down at the table to avoid eye contact with either of them or with each other.

Dan then described his Triangle of Relationship and how people in a relationship try to jostle for the limited space in the control area. He explained how he had dumped his ego and moved out of control to empathy and compassion where Betsy and he now happily co-exist.

"We are not here to give you advice. We cannot; we ourselves are still learning and trying. But as friends who are very fond of you, we want to share our concern. We do not know what is going on, but having known you both for so many years, we can sense all is not well and that you are both very unhappy about it." Dan deliberately skipped any mention of Anne's discussion with Betsy.

"You will have to sort it out yourselves. All we can assure you is that Betsy and I are available twenty-four-seven for any help you may need."

Anne looked up at them with pain and gratitude, restraining the moisture in her eyes. But she could no longer hold them, and tears rolled down her cheeks. Before either of them could react, Karan was out of his chair in a flash, moved to Anne, bent over, and put his arms around her. She held his arms tightly, leaned on one and continued to sob quietly as he tried to comfort her.

Unexpected as it was, Karan's move startled Dan and Betsy and left them rooted to their chairs. With a glint of hope that had suddenly surfaced, their eyes met and gestured that it was time to leave the Chopras alone.

The rest of Sunday was uneventful and moved fast. After leaving the Chopras at the club, they had not tried to contact them. Though both were very curious to find out the outcome, they had agreed that they could do nothing more; the best was to allow them space. The ice was broken; now they had to choose the path.

By dinner time, their curiosity was testing their patience, "What do you think is happening at the Chopras'?" Betsy inquired.

"I hope nothing negative. I guess, as the barrier – should I? would (s)he? – is now broken, they must be sorting things out. We will know only when they choose to involve us."

Just then Betsy's phone rang. It was Anne.

"Hi Betsy. We cannot thank you and Dan enough for your

compassion and friendship. What looked impossible this morning has happened – Karan and I are together, talking. Still some ways to go but a good beginning nevertheless."

Betsy could no longer control her excitement. "I am so happy for you both." She said loudly so that Dan could hear, "Where are you?" and pressed the speaker button.

"We decided to check into the Westin resort for the next two days. We both took a few days off as we did not want mundane things like work to interfere with our new start. I will share details when we meet."

"I called because we know that you would be concerned… and to thank you both. We pray that everyone gets friends like you. God bless you." Intense palpable emotion in her voice.

Betsy's emotions too got the better of her as she groped for words, "Mmm… Thanks for letting us know, Anne. Yes, we were concerned about you. I am delighted that you are both working it out. Best wishes."

"Let's talk when you are back. How about dinner with us on Friday."

"Love to Betsy. Thanks again. Please thank Dan on our behalf. Karan and I are blessed to have you as our friends. Good night."

"Goodnight, Anne. Say hello to Karan. Best wishes and take care."

Betsy hung up with a jubilant look at Dan and found his expressions almost mirroring hers. Simultaneously, they burst out laughing in delight and were joined by the full moon, the quiet night and everything around them.

Strange, how state of mind transforms the surroundings!

FIFTEEN

Dan was up quite early Monday morning. Apart from his scheduled meeting with Tom, he had decided to record his week's learnings in the morning instead of his usual Sunday night. He did not have the heart to leave Betsy alone in the celebratory mood of last night.

He moved to his study. He had to clear his mind as a lot had happened over the weekend. He started to relive the week, starting Monday meeting with Tom.

'The conflict with Tom was resolved in a win-win engagement. He also appeared to be seeking and soaking well. But apparently, he did not sift and share well enough to convert knowledge into learning. It was obvious by his behavior in my leadership team meeting.'

'But he got provoked by Rob as he later explained. People will always say or do something that can offend us. We cannot regulate their actions. What really matters is our response to it, which is within our control. ThERe is the right way, but it requires a lot of maturity and practice. Tom was certainly not ThERe, and his disappointing response showed it. However, isn't it too much to expect him to practice his new knowledge so fast. Am I being unfair? I need to give him more time to learn and practice. The session with him today will be particularly important.'

'I must explain ThERe concept to Tom in a simpler way. How?' and a thought took root. He opened Excel and started to

punch the keys. Ten minutes later he stopped, looked at his work and smiled.

'Yes, that will work.' He thought and printed the file.

'Ron's session was very profound. It had so many learnings. And as luck would have it, I was able to use the Expectations Conundrum almost immediately with Karan and Anne, hopefully with lasting success. Would I have been able to achieve the same result a few weeks back? I doubt it. For one, I would not have the models. But would that be the only difference? Although the model may have played a part, it was only a tool, which I used effectively.'

'What did I do differently? I know for sure that I would have tried to control and persuade Karan and Anne to reconcile. It would not have worked because my persuasion would have probably made them more adamant and would have fed their egos. Yesterday, in place of control and persuasion, they experienced our empathy and compassion that gave them the confidence to lower their guard. That Betsy and I had recently resolved a similar situation successfully must have also been a big influencer. They responded to our compassion with commitment to overcome their egos and embrace each other. So far, it appears that Betsy and I were helpful. I hope they can put their issues behind them for good. Need to thank Ron again.' His thoughts shifted to Ron.

'Ron is incredible. It is clear to me now why he became VP so fast. I have always liked him but now I am a fan. His ability to convert extraordinarily complex issues into simple and easy-to-understand concepts is awe-inspiring. It cannot be done without outstanding clarity of mind. How does one inculcate that? Still a lot to learn!'

'Let me update my learnings.'

He opened the word file, and his fingers began dancing on the keyboard. He reviewed and rewrote previous and new entries a few times until he felt satisfied.

Dan's Learnings

Ron's Success Mantras

VALUE people and empower them for peak performance.

FEEL and THINK first, then Speak or Write, ASK to learn and LISTEN to understand.

Clarify the INTENT before any conversation to prevent misinterpretation.

Forego CONTROL to build and strengthen relationships.

Care for people selflessly to INFULENCE and gain COMMITMENT.

Use conflicts as an opportunity to ENGAGE.

SHARE new knowledge to create applicable LEARNING.

Understand, define, align and meet the needs of every RELATIONSHIP.

He read the list one final time, made some changes to earlier learnings, saved the file, and closed his laptop. He then went back to the bedroom to wake Betsy. He kissed her lightly on the forehead. Before he could say anything, she put her arms around his neck and sleepily murmured, "Good Morning, darling. I was waiting for you. Hope you were able to finish your work. I will get the breakfast while you get ready." And she got out of the bed.

Dan was in the car at seven thirty a.m. sharp.

Tom was waiting when he reached the office. They met enthusiastically and settled down in a huddle room after picking up coffee from the pantry.

Dan chose not to talk about Tom's Friday fiasco. The learning cycle had helped him recognize that converting 'knowledge' to 'learning' and 'practice' was tough and required time and patience. He had far more empathy and understanding towards Tom's behavior now.

He explained the learning cycle and why consistent practice is not possible until knowledge becomes learning, which brought a smile and sigh of relief from Tom. He admitted that he had not been able to spend enough time to assimilate what they had discussed last Monday, and it had been stored preventing the learning. He committed that he would invest sufficient time to share so that he can practice the learnings effectively.

Dan also explained the concept of ThERe, and why 'think before you react' was so critical. He shared his morning creativity with Tom.

"Thanks. I certainly followed the red path last Friday," Tom said, almost apologetically.

"I thought it over the weekend but was somewhat confused about what I could have done differently. It is now clear. I interpreted Rob's question as a threat and went down the red path. Irrespective of his intent, if I had paused and thought, and if I was ThERe, I could have taken it as an opportunity to engage and win-win!"

"I am glad you can see it this way, Tom. It is not easy. We are programmed to react instantly as soon as we perceive a threat. It takes strong commitment and patience to pause. ThERe is the only solution."

"I am totally committed, Dan, driven by your empathy and compassion for me. Thanks again for your time. I really appreciate it. I will see you again next Monday."

Dan had chosen not to share the Conundrum of Expectations as he thought it was probably not relevant for Tom at this stage. But they discussed Expectations Swap and agreed to review and align each other's expectations next Monday.

Tom left with commitment to convert the knowledge to learning and practice it.

'*The morning was well spent. We made a difference today,*' Dan thought.

The rest of the week was busy but quiet.

Dan rushed through completion of his weekly work as the much-anticipated Friday evening approached.

SIXTEEN

Linda was not at her desk when Dan walked into Ron's office. Ron welcomed him with his usual enthusiasm.

Once they settled down, Ron asked, "Dan, last week you asked me how it all comes together. Before I answer that question, it is important that we address a subject that probably brought you to me."

"If I recall correctly, you had said something about several people bypassing you and being made directors. Right?" asked Ron looking at Dan with a smile.

Dan looked blankly at Ron with some embarrassment as he was much wiser by now and had realized the difference between Ron and him.

"Ron, I already have my answer as far as you are concerned. I can't say the same for the few others who bypassed me."

"I realize that Dan, and that is why it is crucial that we discuss this rather openly. I must add, however, that what I say today is as a friend. It is not in my official capacity as your boss' boss or your hierarchical VP."

"I will proceed only if this is okay with you."

"Yes, Ron. I well understand and appreciate it. Thanks for asking."

"Great. Let us start."

"In which areas do we assess employee performance? Before you respond, let me clarify that you know it as well as I, but it is critical that we examine this again."

"We review individual's results and assess his or her strengths and improvement areas. This is reviewed in retrospect. Secondly, we help the individual create a plan for the coming year – actions and targets. Finally, we understand the career interests and help develop his or her individual development plan," Dan replied.

"Thanks for indulging me and stating the obvious. I ask this because there are two significant points I want to make. First, we focus far too much on improvement areas. I am sure you know the reason."

"Yes, Ron," Dan said with a faint smile. "This is our lever to justify why the individual is not yet ready for promotion or large salary increase and we exploit it to the hilt."

Ron did not smile. "Yes. Unfortunately, this is one of the worst parts of our talent development system. Instead of focusing on the strengths of the individual and honing them further, we focus maximum energy of the appraisal on the weaknesses or improvement areas."

"What does this do? It gives a message to the individual that correcting his or her weaknesses is far more important to the company than the strengths. So, the individual starts to spend disproportionate effort in fixing the identified weaknesses, even at the cost of compromising some of his or her strengths. Net result, the company ends up with well-rounded average performers rather than brilliant ones with some rough edges."

"Said another way, our appraisal system is focused on rounding the rough edges of a stone rather than polishing it into a diamond! This is true for almost all companies with probably very few exceptions."

"So true, Ron; I have often wondered about it. In fact, sometimes we 'find' a weakness just so we can fill that box and have a 'meaningful' discussion."

"Don't get me wrong, Dan. I am not suggesting that we ignore critical issues that make an individual less effective. They must be addressed."

"My point is that we must celebrate the brilliance or the strengths of an individual and spend far more time identifying ways to build them further. That does not mean that we ignore the 'opportunity areas' that, if addressed, will make the individual an even better performer."

"No one is perfect – there is always a niggle or rough edge. That will always be. But I would rather have a brilliant performer with some rough edges than an above-average performer who is well-rounded."

Dan's performance appraisals over the years were almost constantly focused around his improvement areas. Except once when Ron was his boss, where the focus was not on his weaknesses but on how to leverage his strengths to step change his contributions and performance. *'It was so different – positive and invigorating experience versus the typical negative dreadful exercise. Ron has always been walking his talk,'* he thought.

"You are right, Ron. The performance appraisal system is a routine that does not inspire."

Ron was uncharacteristically somber and did not comment. He was visibly unhappy about the situation.

"It is important to understand that this prevails in almost all companies across all industries. In fact, The Global Company is better than most and has always believed in continuous improvement. Some of us are currently working with HR leadership to transform and make our appraisal system truly meaningful and a competitive advantage." He finally smiled.

"Ron, another opportunity area is the subjectivity and

ambiguity of our promotion criteria. Making it more consistent and transparent will also help a lot," Dan offered.

"I agree, Dan. However, subjectivity cannot be eliminated from performance rating or appraisal system as people are evaluating people. Although we try to be principle-based, checkboxes cannot work for a system as diverse and complex as talent development, more so at senior hierarchical levels."

"What we lack is the structure to a critical dimension of promotability. What could that be?"

Dan thought for a while, "Is it the ability to perform in the future as we have a pretty good system for contribution assessment," Dan replied.

"I assume you mean 'potential,' and you are absolutely right, Dan."

"A robust talent development system must assess two key parameters – contribution and potential, apart from other things like strengths, opportunity areas, career interests, targets and action plans etc."

"Contribution is tangible and is easy to assess—actual results vis-à-vis the goals and targets. There are sufficient assessment metrics and methodologies. Not so for potential; the challenge begins with definition of potential and goes all the way to its assessment. No wonder, most companies leave it to the direct boss to make a totally subjective assessment of potential."

"This is also the core reason for people dissatisfaction about their promotability." Ron added looking at Dan.

Dan understood what Ron had left unspoken. He did well not to let it show on his face. "How would you define potential, Ron?" he asked instead.

"Dan, I will answer it after we have discussed another important concept. It is not appropriate to counterquestion, but I am sure you will understand. How has your work changed since you joined the company nineteen years-ago?"

'Wow, he knows I joined the company nineteen years back,' Dan's first thought.

"I have progressively spent more time on leadership, which was not the case when I started. In fact, this has made me busier and increased my workload."

"We will talk about leadership a little later. Let's first review this." Ron walked to the whiteboard and drew a picture.

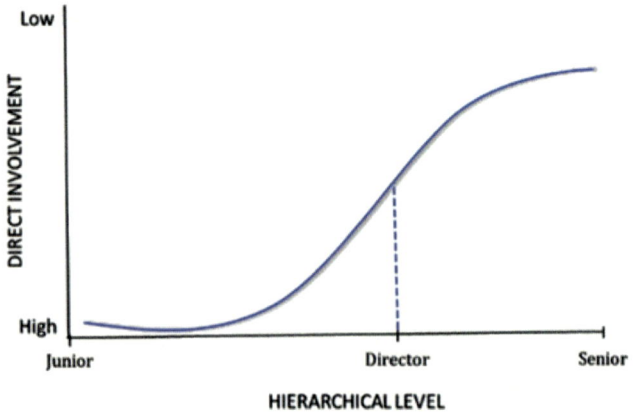

Changing Role With Hierarchical Growth

"Our direct involvement in day-to-day affairs reduces as we move up the hierarchical ladder. The slope of the curve can vary depending upon the individual and the company, but the basic principle is consistent – direct operational involvement reduces as we move higher in the organization. This is because our work and success measures change."

"As our role changes, we must begin to delegate day-to-day operational work to our teams. Leaders who do not delegate are overworked and compromise not only their own effectiveness but also organizational development, performance, and results."

Ron pretended not to see Dan's reaction to his last statement.

Pointing to the chart, Ron continued, "It is important to note that the rise of the curve is steepest at a certain level in every organization. For our company, the success measures and performance expectations change completely at director level."

"The incumbent needs to spend far more time and effort on 'future' strategy and plans versus 'present' and day-to-day operations. This is also the level where the individual requires more leadership and social skills than technical skills."

"The most crucial skill at this level is the ability to engage effectively. Because this role needs to achieve commitment not only from his or her own organization, but more importantly (s)he must manage political pressures and still be able to influence and gain alignment from cross-organization peers and leaders."

This was not new to Dan; he knew this all along. However, he became quite uncomfortable hearing it from Ron, especially because of the context in which he had come to seek help. He was trying to avoid Ron's eyes.

Ron was aware that this was causing turmoil in Dan's head, but he had no option. Dan had to understand it himself and answer this important and unspoken question. Am I ready to make a successful director?

His expressions and tone getting gentler and softer, Ron continued, "Dan, I know you understand leadership skills very well as the company constantly talks about them. We will discuss them briefly a little later. For now, I want to focus on social skills and specifically, the ability to engage effectively."

"What skills do you think are required for it?"

Dan could not control a smile despite his current state of mind as he realized that this question was being asked just to soothe his flayed nerves.

"Ron, this is what you have been explaining and I have been trying to practice over the past few weeks. I actually created something that you may like." His smile broadened and he pulled a sheet out from the folder he had brought with him.

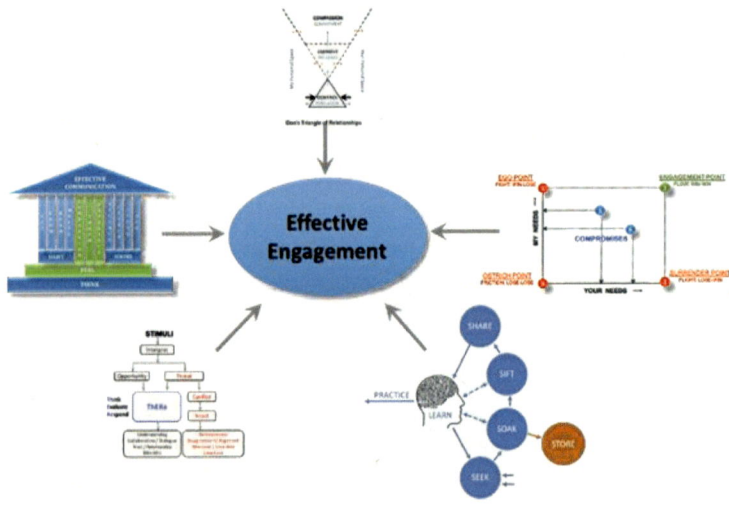

Ron looked at it intently and said with a proud smile, "This is a great summary and pictorial of what we have talked about so far. What is this stimuli picture though? I don't recall seeing it."

Dan, now back to his normal self, was waiting for this question. He handed another sheet to Ron and enthusiastically explained the ThERe model that he had created for Tom.

"Brilliant!" Ron said after reviewing it. "It very well sums up the ThERe concept. It also underlines the importance of what we had earlier discussed—our life is 10% of what happens to us and 90% of how we 'react' to that external stimulus. Very well captured."

"Thanks, Ron," Dan said.

"Another important element your model clearly captures is the choice of interpretation. We can choose to see any event as a threat and go down the red path or view it as an opportunity and follow the blue one."

"You have created a very powerful training module, Dan. Don't forget my royalty though!" he added laughing.

"Coming back to the subject, would you now like to redefine 'potential.'"

"I would say, it is the ability of the individual to be successful in the future. But it is still ambiguous and subjective."

"Yes, it is. That is why it is crucial to define potential. This definition can be different for every company because it must sync with the company's values and purpose. Even within our company, people will describe potential differently as corporate definition does not exist. So, what is potential?"

"First, it is important to recognize what it is not. I exclude technical skills and competence as they get covered under contribution; performance and results."

"Secondly, part of what I am about to describe as potential here may be included as contribution for some senior positions."

"To me, potential of an individual covers three core elements:
1. **Mindful Attitude**
2. **Bold Leadership**
3. **Social Intelligence**

"Do you have a question?" Ron asked, reading Dan's nonverbal, inquisitive expression.

"Yes, I do. What is the difference between mindful versus positive attitude?"

"Good question, Dan. Mindful attitude is neither positive nor negative; it is the attitude of awareness, thoughtfulness, compassion, and trust."

"Let's take an example that may be close to home for you. When you came to me with your request a few weeks back, I had three options. I could have said sorry Dan, I will not be able to help you. Your boss, Joe Bird, is the best person for it. What attitude would that be?"

"I think, it would have been negative attitude."

"Absolutely. Alternatively, I could have answered your question in our first meeting, within an hour. You may not have agreed with my answer, but you would have found it honest, reasonable, and partly convincing. How would you describe that attitude?"

Dan thought for a while and as understanding dawned, he slowly answered. "Positive attitude. Thanks, Ron, I got it."

"The way you have treated my request is because of your mindful attitude. I understand the difference now and it is stark!" said Dan with thankfulness in his voice and nonverbals.

"Please don't misunderstand me. I would most likely never take the first option with anyone. But I would also not take the last option with everyone. I chose to do it for you with an awareness and careful thought."

"It is clear, and I cannot thank you enough for choosing a mindful attitude for me. It has transformed my life."

"No need to thank me, Dan. It has continued for so many weeks because of you and your mindful attitude of learning. Your immense seek, soak, sift and share has inspired me to keep going. I would have ended it much earlier, otherwise."

"Can I ask you another question? I understand leadership as defined in our company but what is bold leadership?"

"Please hold this question for now. Let us first understand **Mindful Attitude**."

"Psychology books and dictionaries are filled with numerous definitions of attitude. I, however, see it rather simply. **Our attitude is the 'values' that drive and guide our behavior and actions**."

"I believe that people with a mindful attitude practice three values:

"**COMPASSION:** Thoughtful understanding and sensitivity to others' needs. Selfless concern and care for others.

"**POSITIVITY:** Acute awareness and grasp of the situation and surroundings. Consistently approaching each problem as an opportunity.

"**TRUST:** Demonstrating confidence in capability and intentions of others. Consistent, dependable, and predictable behavior.

"I consider the two behaviors described under each value to be the critical ones. More can be added by others as appropriate based on individual experiences and beliefs."

"Very clear. Do individual values have to align with the company's?" asked Dan.

"Ideally yes, but not necessarily. However, if personal and corporate values conflict, one must either find a way to align them or look for a change. It will otherwise be difficult to succeed in the company."

"Let us now answer your earlier question. Leadership is probably the most used corporate word. I qualify it with 'bold' – bold leadership."

"Bold means creating a vision that challenges, inspires, engages, and energizes. Bold means developing stretching, time-bound objectives and goals and choosing the right strategies to deliver them. Bold means predicting and building required people, system, and process capabilities. Bold means getting 'more with less.' Bold means anticipating and leading change to create and sustain competitive advantage. Bold means confidence to take informed risks. Bold means making timely decisions using data as well as gut. Bold means not only laser-like focus on the work to deliver aligned objective and goals but standing up to say NO to things that may divert or distract the resources."

"Bold does not mean fearless or reckless but courageous, knowledge-based leadership, rooted in some core skills." A bold leader is:

VISIONARY: The ability to develop challenging vision, goals and enabling strategies. The ability to engage, enroll, and energize the organization/team in pursuit of these strategies, and focus them only on value-added work.

ENTREPRENUER: The ability to courageously integrate both data and intuition and dare to take informed risks. The ability to create opportunities and learning experiences from tough situations and failures.

TRANSFORMER: The ability to embrace changing environment and take personal responsibility to anticipate and lead change. The ability to aggressively search, share, and reapply knowledge through healthy dissatisfaction with status quo.

COACH: The ability to identify, recognize, and fully utilize inherent capabilities of each individual. Value and leverage their diverse experiences and skills. The ability to inspire individuals and teams through experiential learning/knowledge and enable them to exceed expectations, standards, and goals.

"Does this answer your question, Dan?"

"It does but I do not see **Collaborator**, something that the company constantly reminds us that a good leader must be?"

"Excellent question!" Ron said with a purposeful smile. "Does inclusion of collaboration within leadership skills make you act differently, Dan?"

"Yes. As collaboration is currently a key leadership skill for the company, I develop the vision and the strategies to ensure that they are acceptable to others." Dan replied.

"Would your vision and strategies be different if collaboration was not part of the company's leadership skill?" Ron questioned.

"Yes. They would be far more stretching and challenging."

"I think you just answered your question. But allow me to elaborate further."

"Recall when we earlier talked about leveraging strengths rather than weaknesses. It is somewhat similar. We tend to round-off key skills. So, we add 'collaboration' as a core leadership skill to counterbalance its 'assertiveness.'"

"Does it make us, the leaders, deliver better results? I am afraid not. We compromise and temper down our vision/objective/goals/strategies to make them acceptable to all."

"I see it differently." continued Ron, "Bold leaders must be aggressive. Counterbalance for me comes not from compromising leadership skills but from the synergistic effect of other 'potential' skills. Mindful attitude and social intelligence balance the aggressiveness of bold leadership."

"Thanks, Ron. It makes lot of sense to me."

"Moving to Social Intelligence. It is all that we have talked about in the past few weeks. The outcome of social intelligence skills is effective engagement. The ability to communicate effectively, ability to influence and gain commitment, ability to share and learn, ability to be ThERe, ability to prevent conflict or get to a win-win resolution quickly, and the ability to build, strengthen and preserve relationships."

"The potential of an individual is the synergistic effect of all three: Mindful Attitude, Bold Leadership and Social Intelligence."

"An individual's true performance is a combination of this potential and contribution."

"Dan, has the ambiguity and subjectiveness reduced now?"

"It certainly has, Ron. Ambiguity is gone. Subjectivity has come down significantly but cannot be eliminated as you said earlier. This is a good framework for performance evaluation. The only question for me is how do we measure and track this subjective 'potential?'"

"Great question. The Behavior Observation System (BOS) is probably the best way to do it. As a first step, we will need to define the desired behaviors under values and skills of each potential element. For example, key behaviors under visionary skill, for me, are:

"VISIONARY

"Recognizing the opportunities presented by business needs.

"Creating challenging vision and consequent goals, strategies that would leverage these opportunities and exceed expectations of our external customers to create unsurmountable competitive advantage.

"Engaging, enrolling, and energizing others in pursuit of these vision, goals, and strategies.

"Focusing only on the work and ask only for the work that adds value to the aligned goals, and strategies.

"Once desired behaviors are defined and deployed for each

value and skill, a 360-degree assessment needs to be conducted involving the individual (self-assessment), his or her boss, cross-organizational peers, and direct reports. All of them will rate the individual on observed frequency of these desired behaviors (Always, Often, Rarely, Never); a numeric value, four for always and zero for never, is assigned to each. Score for each value and skill should be cumulated and averaged for each key element of potential. The scores for all three elements can be averaged to create the final 'potential score.'"

"Wow! This can be immensely powerful, Ron." Dan asked, "Are we planning to introduce it in the company?"

"I cannot answer this, Dan. I am trying my best to get it implemented using every skill I have."

Dan asked, "So, where do we go from here?"

Ron walked to his desk and picked up a sheet.

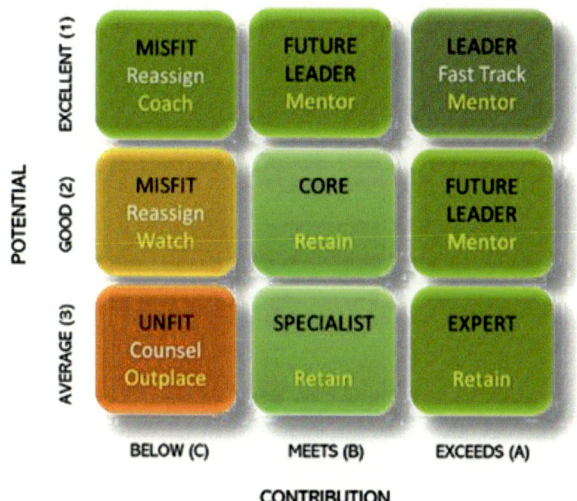

PERFORMANCE MATRIX

"Many companies use variations of this performance matrix. But almost all assess 'potential' subjectively."

Before Ron could go further, Dan interjected. He could no longer resist, "Where do you see me fit, Ron?"

"I am sorry, Dan. I hope you can understand my inability to answer your question. As I had requested earlier, I am not speaking to you in my official capacity. It is Joe Bird's prerogative to provide your performance assessment. I can neither intervene nor circumvent it. Besides, this is not a system that The Global Company is using."

"But I think you now know enough. You can self-evaluate to determine where you currently fit and where you would like to be."

"Sorry for asking. I understand, Ron." Dan said apologetically.

"The key point you should remember," said Ron pointing to the sheet, "It is sexy to be 1A and be labelled LEADER, but the employees in many other boxes are equally valuable, and often preferred. They are more loyal, lesser retention risk and form the organizational backbone."

"What do you think box 1C is, Dan?"

"Excellent potential but contribution below expectations. I think they are a square peg in a round hole, meaning they are probably in a wrong role and should be reassigned."

"Well said. Do you know what our appraisal system does to such people?"

Dan thought for a while, "As earlier discussed, we keep identifying and focusing on their weaknesses to justify their poor contribution. And make them 2C or 2B."

"Unfortunately, true in most cases. Instead of reassigning them to a role that will fit and hone their skills and strengths, we try to smoothen the 'square peg' to fit in the 'round hole.' This not only wastes the talent and potential of the individual but also interferes in their career development."

"If we do it right, people in all boxes other than 3C, can move eastward through coaching and focused assignment planning."

"Moving northward and improving 'potential' is far more difficult. That is why company recruitment systems put higher value on the potential of the candidates, albeit in a subjective way. It is done for two other reasons. First, it is impossible to assess the contributions of an individual in a one-hour interview. Second, subjective assessment of the 'potential' can provide an indication if the individual can fit within the company culture."

"I too have always given higher weight to 'potential' because I consider it difficult to teach and learn these skills. Contribution improvement, on the other hand, can be guided through coaching and training."

"However, thanks to your learning cycle model and the outstanding progress you have demonstrated on social intelligence skills in such a short time, I will have to reconsider my belief." Ron said laughing and raised his hands up as if in surrender. His eyes caught sight of his wristwatch by chance.

"Goodness. It is quite late. Let's call it a day. I would not want to interfere with your work-life balance." He laughed again.

"It is not an issue with me, Ron. But if you have a few more minutes, can I ask you another question now that this topic has come up?"

"Sure, Dan. Please go ahead."

"What do you think of this newfound focus on work-life balance?"

"In all humility, I must say that it is a symptom of a bigger, but unconnected problem. It is complicated but I will try to explain as simply as I can."

"Instead of being the passion, work is often seen as a compulsion for sustenance. We discussed some of the possible reasons earlier today."

"Second, globalization has taken away the sanctity of workhours, especially in regional or global roles; an office is always operating somewhere in the world twenty-four-seven! And while we are at home, someone may be looking for our help somewhere in the company. Further, global calls are always at an inconvenient time for one or the other region."

"Third, technology has made our work location-free; what was earlier confined to and had to be completed only within the four walls of our workplace, has now creeped into our homes. We no longer care if it remains unfinished; in fact, we often shelve it for home."

"Finally, our innate desire to be aware of and on top of everything, keeps us watching our smartphones constantly."

"So, although we are physically at home with our families, our mind is somewhere else; we are still involved with work issues. This, to me, is the 'work-life balance' issue in a nutshell."

"Some issues are inherent and difficult to solve but most can be. Those who love and cherish what they do, find innovative ways to devote quality time to it. They are far more productive and can easily switch off when they leave office. Once we find quality time for work in the office and quality time for family at home, no imbalance. We are in harmony."

"You are right. I too was one of those balance-seekers earlier. I was physically at home, but not really there. So, while my inbox was always squeaky clean, my personal life had far too much clutter. Ever since I embarked on this new journey, the need for balance has vanished. When I am with Betsy, I am 100%

there. Surprisingly, there is no negative effect on my work; contrarily, my productivity and work life has improved."

"I am so glad that you are benefiting in so many ways, Dan. I have not come across such a fast learner before. It is truly remarkable."

"So, what say? We call it a day?" asked Ron.

Dan nodded and started to gather his things.

"Have a great weekend. Say hello to Betsy. We must catch up someday soon."

"Thanks, Ron. Would love to. Have a nice weekend and goodnight."

They shook hands and Dan left Ron's office thoughtfully quiet.

'Hasn't Ron already answered my promotability question without saying a word? I probably fit the bottom right box in the potential-contribution matrix.'

The thought was sobering. He had begun to realize and accept his inability to make a director, but the structured understanding of the reasons was disappointing.

His emotions were muddled up; the happiness through achievement of past few weeks left no place for negativity, but a hint of sadness had now creeped in.

'I need to face the reality. This is the truth. At least I know now. Wasn't this the very reason that took me to Ron? In fact, I am blessed to have learned so much that has changed my life. Knowing the truth often hurts but fighting it prolongs the pain. I must accept it and celebrate that I not only know what needs to be done but am already practicing it, noticeably as everyone, including Ron, has remarked.

The last thought brought some comfort and he relaxed. That is when he realized that he was already in his driveway. He had not been conscious of the last thirty minutes – leaving office, getting in the car, and driving home happened intuitively without real awareness.

He parked the car and walked inside through the garage door. Anne greeted him with a huge smile.

SEVENTEEN

Betsy and Dan had decided not to ask any questions about last week unless it was brought up by the Chopras. They were delighted to see Anne and Karan back in the old spirits, literally. A few days together had made a huge difference; they had not only resolved the conflict, but they seemed closer and happier. It was evident in their tipsy responses to each other.

Drinks and dinner were the usual joyful and noisy fest, as if last week never existed. Post dinner, they all retired to the garden sipping the exclusive wine Betsy had bought for the occasion. Karan spoke.

"Anne has talked to Betsy, but I have not had a chance to thank you both for your understanding, patience, and your friendship. Your mediation was perfect – you intervened without intrusion, giving us space to think, reflect and realize the absurdity of our behaviors. It also made us recognize that we value our relationship far more than the appetite of our egos. We don't have words to thank you."

Anne was nodding her agreement.

"We are delighted to see you both smiling, together!" remarked Dan.

"Thanks, Dan. I feel so bad and cannot excuse myself, the so-called psychology professor, to let my ego run amok. Not sure if this is the appropriate time to talk about my values but it may probably help you too as it complements your Conundrum of Expectations model."

"We would love to hear, Karan." Betsy and Dan said in unison.

"We believe in the concept of impermanence or '*Anitya*' in Sanskrit; everything in the universe is transient and will cease to exist; what is born will die. While I know my end is inevitable, when and how my journey will end is unknown to me. I do not know if I will get an opportunity to say, 'I love you, Anne' tomorrow. The only thing '*Nitya*' or permanent, is the present moment while it lasts. And I have a choice – either I seize it to do or say what truly matters to me or rue over it. Tomorrow may or may not be for me!"

"Alas, knowledge that remains unutilized, is worse than ignorance. Therefore, I am so upset with myself."

He paused and looked at their mesmerized faces.

Dan was tempted to explain his learning cycle but knew the inappropriateness of the moment. Instead, he said, "I know what you mean. It is the lose-lose ostrich behavior, just to appease one's ego."

"Yes, Dan. Ego it was."

"Impermanence of the body is accepted in most cultures, but we also believe in permanence of the real self, '*Atman*' in Sanskrit; while the body along with its ego decays, the spirit or soul is eternal and indestructible. Sadly, I allowed my impermanent ego to take control of my permanent self!" Anguish was clearly visible on his face.

Anne was watching him with pride and passion.

"Thanks for explaining this wonderful Indian belief, Karan. It is really fascinating and a clear reminder of what not to do," Betsy said.

"For now, let us seize this '*Nitya*' moment to celebrate our success in conquering our egos and surrender to our '*Atman*.' Did

I get the concept correct, Karan?"

"Brilliantly, Betsy." Karan applauded.

They started talking of more mundane things. Excited voices and constant laughter kept the night awake.

After the Chopras left past eleven p.m., Dan and Betsy cleaned up and sat down.

"I liked the *Anitya* concept very much. We really have no idea how much time we have left together. Can we agree that we will continue to seize every *Nitya* moment as we have done in the past few weeks?" asked Betsy.

"Exactly what I was thinking, Bet. I want to go a step further though. I have a proposition – if ever an issue leads us to a rift, can we both commit to forget it by next morning and begin the day afresh with usual hugs and kisses?" "This morning dose of oxytocin will melt away bitterness of the previous day and strengthen our love and passion for each other."

Betsy's response was electric, "That will be fantastic, Dan. I am fully committed. But I want to make it interesting. Whoever does not honor this pledge will have to buy a bottle of wine that the other person chooses; no price restrictions!" She said with a canny smile.

Dan laughed, "Done. With our skin in the game now, we may at least get to drink some nice expensive wines."

Betsy added, "This may help us move towards the 'expectation-free relationship.' I love it."

On that happy note they decided it was time for bed.

The weekend was short and over rather quickly. Dan excused himself to his study on Sunday night. Betsy was expecting it and had lined up other things for herself.

Dan had mixed emotions about his last session with Ron. Although he understood the reasons, Ron's refusal to comment on his performance, yet giving a clear message without saying a word, was disappointing to say the least.

'Why should it disappoint me? I was aware of and had already accepted this outcome long back.'

He was not able to understand and had no answer. Probably he was expecting Ron to confirm his theory that the company had been unfair to him. Instead, without saying it, Ron had emphatically explained why Dan was not yet ready to become director. Perhaps that was the pain-point. Spoken or unspoken, truth hurts!

Other than this temporary disillusionment, Dan was quite satisfied and happy with his learnings and progress over the past few weeks.

His thoughts moved to the contribution-potential matrix, and its rating. He knew that his contribution level was comparable to the best. The challenge was potential, which had never been explained to him so succinctly. More importantly, Ron's suggested quantifiable rating system had appealed to his analytical left brain. With trepid excitement he started self-evaluation on Ron's potential criteria:

*'On **Social Intelligence**, my rating will be low as I am still discovering and learning through Ron's sessions. Although I have started making progress, I still have a long way to go. Numerically, I would rate myself '2' out of 5.'*

He rated himself '2' on mindful attitude as well, using the same logic.'

*'I think I am a good leader as several of my bosses have told me over the years, but where do I fit on the **Bold Leadership** metric?*

He recalled the four skills of bold leadership that Ron had described and entered them in an Excel spreadsheet. He also entered Ron's suggested behaviors for visionary skill as best as he could recall.

'I will later define the suitable behaviors for each of these skills as Ron had advised. For now, let me rate against Ron's proposed behaviors for visionary, and overall score for each of the other skills.' He decided.

Bold Leadership: Visionary
Recognize the opportunities posed by business needs.
'I would rate '1' as I have spent little to no time to understand business needs.'
Create challenging vision and corresponding strategies that would leverage these opportunities to exceed the expectations and create competitive advantage.
'Rate '2''. 'I do this well except for the customer and consumer connection, which should be the starting point.'
Engage, enroll, and energize others in pursuit of these visions and strategies.
'Rate '1''. 'This is a significant opportunity area for me.'
Focus only on the work and ask only for the work that adds value to the aligned goals, and strategies.
'Rate '2''. 'I am unable to say no when some work pops up.'
He averaged one and a half out of five on visionary skill.
'God! I thought I was better than this.
Bold Leadership: Entrepreneur. *'Rate '3''. 'I am innovative and decisive. I always look for execution quality and excellence. But I am not a risk-taker.*
Bold Leadership: Transformer. *'Rate '2''. My change leadership is an opportunity. I am also far too accepting, and dissatisfaction with the status quo has gone. I no longer challenge it.'*

Bold Leadership: Coach. *'Rate '1''. 'I am improving but I do not delegate well enough. I prefer to do things myself directly rather than spend time on coaching.'*

He noted his average bold leadership score.

'1.97 is my overall Potential score. Very disappointing! I have got my answer!'

"I commit to take it above 3.0 within the next quarter," Dan said loudly in a determined voice.

The celebratory mood of the weekend had been replaced by an unwavering resolve.

EIGHTEEN

Tom was waiting when Dan reached his office Monday morning.

After pleasantries and a cup of coffee, they both settled down in the huddle room. Tom shared the progress he had made over the week, which was quite impressive. They then swapped their expectations.

Expectations Swap and Alignment

What Tom expects from Dan?
Coaching and Personal Development
Champion my Promotion
Understand my POV in a controversy
Fair and equitable assessment

What Tom thinks Dan expects from him?
Outstanding Organizational Results
Compliance with company policies
Trust and Loyalty
Retention

Expectations Swap and Alignment

What Dan Expects from Tom?
On time delivery of all targets and projects

Total transparency and openness
Organization and People development
Personal development

What Dan thinks Tom expects from him?
Coaching and Mentoring
Challenging assignments
Resource allocation
Promotion

After reviewing Tom's expectations from him, Dan asked. "What do you think, Tom? Are we aligned?

"No, Dan. There is a mismatch. For example, I think you expect from me **trust and loyalty**, **retention**, and **compliance**. These do not find a place on your list. Instead, you expect from me **openness and transparency**, **organization and people development**, and **personal development**. This is a revelation."

"That is the very reason for this exercise; to bring us on the same page."

"We will need to work these. The important thing to understand is that we have so far been guessing what the other expects. And because our guesses are inaccurate, we have often disappointed each other. Let's set up a separate session for understanding and aligning our expectations. I plan to do it with the whole leadership team. I will also recommend that all of you do it with each other."

Tom nodded, "It is a good idea, Dan." He looked quite uncomfortable though. The reason became apparent to Dan soon.

"I would have let Human Resources inform you, but in the spirit of total transparency that you expect from me, I think it is appropriate for me to tell you now; Amy Brown has resigned."

"Isn't she our best and top-rated department manager?" Dan asked.

"Yes." Tom replied regretfully.

"What happened? Do we know why she wants to leave? How can we retain her?" Dan fired several questions.

"I had a long chat with her. I wanted to understand it prior to her exit-interviews with you and HR." Tom paused.

He looked even more uncomfortable. "She thinks she is not getting adequate freedom to operate." Anxiousness written all over his face, Tom continued hesitantly, "That I micromanage her, which she doesn't like." Tom avoided meeting Dan's eyes.

Dan had to exercise immense self-control to manage his nonverbals and the anger that had begun to build inside. He thought of ThERe and said to himself, *'I must treat this as an opportunity, not a threat. Think, evaluate and respond.'* The pause was making Tom even more uneasy.

Dan finally spoke, unemotionally, "Recall the ThERe model we discussed last Monday. Let's treat this as an opportunity, instead of a threat. We can discuss Amy a little later. For now, I want to share something with you."

Tom nodded. There was nothing else he could think of.

"As you must be aware, micromanagement has also been my opportunity. You may have noticed that I have been able to avoid it in the past few weeks."

"How could I do it? It has taken lots of thinking. I found that I was micromanaging to prevent failures because my trust in team's capability was low. I also found that as a result, I was absolving the team members of accountability and ownership of their work."

"What did that do?"

Tom interjected. "You alienated us, increasing the chances

of failures. In fact, there have been far too many fires to douse, that should have been prevented in the first place." He was more composed now after his boss' confession to the same problem.

"Thanks, Tom. Yes, absolutely! I have now started to hold all of you accountable; and now I coach rather than micromanage, wherever I see a capability gap or a miss on expected results. I hope you noticed."

"Yes. We all have, and it has been such a refreshing change for all of us."

"Great," said Dan. "Secondly, as we move up the hierarchy, our roles change. At your level, you need to find the right balance between direct involvement in day-to-day work and getting the work done through others; lead and delegate. As yours is the first leadership level, it sometimes becomes difficult to find that balance."

"Letting go is tough. We have far more confidence in our own abilities than others. We often find it easier and faster to do it ourselves than coach and delegate, which is time consuming."

"Yes, we do. But this is a critical skill for us to move up the hierarchical ladder. How else can we build organization capability?"

Tom was quiet as he clearly heard another reason why he was not yet ready to make associate director.

"I understand Dan and am committed to make amends."

"Let's now discuss Amy. What do you think we should do?"

"We cannot lose her, Dan. She is brilliant; probably one of the best young managers in the company. Unfortunately, she seemed quite determined to leave. She has a section manager offer from another global company."

"As she is already on our promotion list, we can promote and assign her to Project Polaris as that role is still open."

"I have different plans for that project, Tom. But it is a good idea. I will consider it. We need to act quickly before she commits to that company. Next steps?"

"I have already spoken to her, Dan. Her Performance Review and Enhancement Plan (PREP) is also ready with me. As the secondary reviewer of PREP, you can meet her and take it from there. What do you think?"

"Good idea. Can I see her later today or tomorrow? I will free up my calendar as this is particularly important. Please have her set it up with Anita. I will brief her."

"Coming back to you, how are other things, Tom. How is the conversion of knowledge to learning?"

"I think I am making good progress. In fact, even Amy told me that she has noticed a change but unfortunately, it is too late for her."

"The only hiccup is work-life balance as I have been spending a lot of time assimilating my knowledge even at home. Tara feels ignored and somewhat upset. We will get over it in due course, I guess."

Dan gave his best knowledge-based smile and explained what Ron had told him last Friday. He also shared his personal learnings.

"Tom, it is not how much time we spend at work or home, but how we spend that time! You can be at home twenty-four-seven but if you are constantly thinking about work, you will still have no time for Tara and yourself. Result, work-life imbalance."

"Work-life balance issues will vanish if we can devote quality time to whatever we do and forget home when at work and forget work when at home. If you must take some work-related matters home, which is very possible in today's digital world, align with Tara transparently. She will not mind your short absence as long as you are 100% with her at other times."

"This is very helpful. I will start implementation today."

"Great. If it's okay with you Tom, let's catch up again next Monday."

"I look forward to it." They shook hands and Tom was on his way.

Dan went back to his desk. Anita reminded him of the upcoming schedule as soon as he got there. He told Anita that Amy Brown would call to schedule a meeting with him, "It is a priority. Please free up my calendar as I want to see her as soon as possible."

Dan had a busy day. After lunch Anita informed him that Amy was scheduled to meet with him tomorrow at eight a.m. He thanked her and went to his next meeting.

He was at work seven fifty a.m. on Tuesday. Amy came into his office at eight a.m. sharp. Dan walked to her and greeted her enthusiastically.

"Morning Amy. How are you today? Can I get you something from the pantry?"

"Good morning, Dan. Thanks. I will join you."

They walked to the pantry together.

Once they were settled in the huddle room, Dan inquired about her parents and when she last met them.

"They are doing good. They came to see me last weekend."

"Must have been a nice weekend." Dan smiled.

"You must be wondering why I want to see you. Tom sent me your project NG report yesterday. I was impressed with the clarity of your thought and the innovative proposal. It takes our Produce-to-Demand effort to a totally different level. Please help me understand the reasons for proposing such an unconventional approach."

Amy's nonverbals changed, and she could not conceal a smile. "Dan, I have researched many Next Generation Supply Chain plans. Almost all of them prioritize one or at best two out of the four critical supply chain vectors – cost, cash, service, agility. In today's competitive world, I think we need at least three; it is not either or. My proposed model optimizes three and inventory. It will not be easy but can be done as I have demonstrated in the report."

"It is a breakthrough. If project NG is successful, we will reapply broadly to other product lines as well. I want you to present your proposal and model in Joe's leadership team next week. I have you on the agenda."

Watching Amy's nonverbals and noticing excitement in her eyes, Dan continued, "We wanted you to lead project NG, but I was disappointed to learn that you want to move on. Can I help the situation in any way?"

Amy thought for a few seconds. "I spoke to Tom. I have learned a lot from him, but I am beginning to feel somewhat stifled. Tom is a brilliant and extraordinarily strong leader, and sometimes the pressure of schedule forces him to compromise coaching in favor of direct involvement."

'Good job, Amy. She is better than I had been told. Certainly, I am witnessing mindful attitude; she has explained Tom's micromanagement problem without a single word against the boss. In fact, she is praising him. Is she the 'star' on our contribution-potential matrix?' He thought.

"What if you are given independent charge of project NG with responsibility for broad scale deployment of your concept 'restaurant-like-flexibility' in supply chain across the category, and probably the company?"

"I would love it, Dan." Amy replied without hesitation,

"There is nothing I would like more than proving my concept and getting it ready for broad scale reapplication."

Now that Amy had agreed to stay because of her passion for the project, Dan did not mind sharing the next good news. He had held it back because he wanted Amy's decision to be independent of this materialistic inducement.

"We will promote you to section manager in the new role."

"Thank you. I really appreciate it. A promotion will be nice but leading my dream project excites me more. Thanks for giving me the opportunity, Dan." Amy replied with a shy smile.

"I am delighted that you have decided to stay, Amy. Please do not share this with anyone. We will soon make an announcement. Thanks again and best wishes," Dan said.

"It is my pleasure."

As Amy walked away, Dan started thinking.

'Is there a learning for me? The assignment to lead project NG has excited her more than the promotion!'

He could not spend any more time on the subject as he was interrupted by Anita. He had to rush for his next meeting.

The rest of the week moved at the speed that is famously The Global Company copyright.

NINETEEN

Dan had an inkling that today may be his last session with Ron. Although he knew of their impermanence, he was saddened that the sessions would be coming to an end.

'I will miss these sessions immensely. I look forward to them so eagerly. But it had to come to an end. Wonder what we will talk about today?'

He shrugged the question away. He did not want to guess and ruin the surprise that came with each session. But he was curious how Ron would wrap it up.

As he walked towards Ron's office, he was nervous. Apart from the apprehension of the impending end of the sessions, he was anxious about today's outcome. Last Friday's session was a bit unsettling.

Linda returned Dan's affectionate smile and waved him in. Ron greeted him with the usual enthusiasm. Once they settled down, Ron began.

"How has the week been, Dan?"

"Very interesting and exciting week. I conducted Expectations Swap with one of my managers and found conflicting expectations. The first learning is that it is not just the swap, aligning the expectations is far more important."

"It certainly is, Dan. What else?"

"I witnessed the impact of excess control by a boss on a brilliant young manager. Luckily, I got a chance to intervene in time. Otherwise, we were heading for a significant regrettable loss, that too of a high potential manager. I also learned that a challenging assignment excites people far more than the promotion."

"Excellent learning. People who focus on action, will always respond this way. We will discuss this a lot more later today. Anything else?"

"Yes. The last and the biggest learning is that I am much worse in all three potential skills versus what I had presumed."

"Don't fret over it. It is understandable. You should feel good that you have made noticeable progress once you became aware. Hopefully, you will have more learnings today."

After a short pause, Ron continued. "Two weeks back you asked me how it all comes together. I had then deferred it for a later day. Today is that day. But before we get to that question, let us explore what brought you to me."

Not waiting for an answer, Ron continued.

"You had told me that you were dissatisfied with your stagnation and did not understand why some people, who you thought were less competent than you, got promoted ahead of you. Did I summarize it correctly?"

"Yes, that was my original question. But I think I have already understood the reason. It is now vividly clear to me why I have not made it so far," Dan said.

"Let me now ask you a more difficult question. Why do you want to get promoted? And I request you to please be ThERe before you reply. I am willing to wait."

A long pause followed.

Dan was surprised that he had to struggle to answer this seemingly simple question.

'*Why do I want to get promoted? The answer should have been obvious as I have wanted it for so long. Why can't I answer* it?'

'Is it for more money? No, money is not the issue; it never was. Is it fairness and true recognition of my work? That probably is the reason.'

When he spoke, Dan's voice was inaudible. He had to clear his throat. "I had never thought of it earlier, but I did not realize that it would be so difficult to answer this question. I guess my desire for promotion is in the spirit of fairness and recognition of my contributions."

"Take your time," Ron said. "My submission is that fairness and recognition of your contributions is your 'want.' What is the 'need' behind this want? But if this is the need, let us understand how and why."

Dan had to think hard. *'Is it a want or the need? I certainly want to get promoted. But what is the need? It is not money. Is it recognition? Not sure if that is true either. Is it peer pressure to prove to them that the company values me? Damn, I am really confused. Let me think aloud.'*

"Although I have always wanted to get promoted, I have never thought about the reason why; it has just been a given. Even now, I cannot figure out what is the need. I know I want to be promoted but the 'why' is unclear. I am sure it is not money. I am uncertain if recognition is the 'need' either. I think, it boils down to being valued; a promotion would signify that the company values my contributions."

"I understand the dilemma," Ron said. "It is not easy to separate want from need for something that is so personal like a promotion. Your thought of 'being valued' as the need, seems quite plausible. The important question, however, is why would you like to be valued? In other words, is being valued also a want and the need something different?"

Dan was stumped, again. *'Why did I so desperately want to get promoted? Why was I unhappy when I was bypassed by my peers and juniors multiple times? Did I want to get promoted to show others my worth? Was it for my ego satisfaction? What was the real need? If being valued is a want, what need is driving it?'*

Confusion and frustration started to show on Dan's face.

'How can I not know why I want to get promoted, something that I have wanted for so many years and has tormented me for so long?'

Realizing his predicament, Ron asked, "Do you want to talk this through, Dan?"

"I never realized that this would be such a difficult question." Dan said almost apologetically.

"You are no exception. Most of us are in the same boat. We desperately want something without knowing why – the need. And this desperation makes us behave and act in a manner that takes us away from the very need," Ron said.

"The more I think about it, it seems to me that I want to get promoted because that is the current yardstick of success. My need was to demonstrate that I am successful."

"Very good. We are now making progress. Let's assume the need is 'demonstration of success'. But, to whom, Dan?" Ron asked gently.

"To my colleagues, to my friends, to my family and to myself, I guess."

"So, you believe that you and everyone around you will think you are successful if you become director in the Global Company. Did I understand it correctly, Dan?"

"I guess so." Dan replied without much conviction.

"I am sorry to be persistent, but it is very important. What is it that makes you and others think that you are not successful now; you are already an associate director. Only a small percentage of employees make AD in our company. What will change if you are director?"

Ron was aware that this question made Dan even more uncomfortable. So instead of waiting for the reply he added, "Once you become a director, wouldn't you and others feel the same about becoming vice president?"

"I don't know." Dan mumbled and continued in a feeble voice, "I guess I will never make a VP. So, that question will not arise."

"Probably for you. But what about others? Everyone knows that vice president is a higher position than director. What stops them from thinking that Dan is not successful as he did not make VP at the Global Company?"

He drilled it in further. "Secondly, you say, and I paraphrase – 'I will never make VP, so it does not bother me.' What about director? You think you can make director?"

Dan had suddenly begun to feel very hot. Each question was fueling his discomfort. He forced himself to be audible when he spoke, "I did, Ron, before I came to you for help. But the past few weeks have made me realize that I am not yet ready."

"But what about others. What will they think? Are you no longer concerned about your colleagues, friends, and family thinking that you are not successful?"

Trying hard to gain composure, Dan paused, in thought. Ron waited patiently, an encouraging smile on his face.

When Dan finally spoke, he had calmed down and regained his poise. "Ron, as I am now convinced that I am not yet ready for a promotion, what others may think is somewhat meaningless and irrelevant."

"Brilliant! Allow me to paraphrase what you just said. I

heard you say that whether I am successful or not can only be determined by me. What others think is irrelevant. Correct?"

"Yes," Dan said. "But I said it with reference to this specific issue of promotion. I am not sure whether I can broaden it to cover everything. How can we isolate ourselves from what people think of us? Are accolades from others just to feed our ego? It is rather confusing."

"I can understand the dilemma. It is a good time to understand success. What do you think is success?"

Dan hesitated. "It is difficult to define, Ron. A close family friend told me that in several Asian countries, success is measured not through your personal achievements but by what you helped your children achieve. Success means different things to different people."

"Exactly! If success means different things to different people, how can anyone from outside verify if I am successful? The only way they can determine it is based on what they see, which is tangible – what you do, where you live, what you drive. Or your telltale soft signals – what you say, and how you act and behave. You can live in the most expensive mansion and drive the fanciest cars but if your words, actions, and behavior portray discontent and dissatisfaction, I doubt if people will consider you successful."

"Ron, are you suggesting that our accumulated wealth has no relationship to success?"

"No, Dan. I am saying that it is you who makes yourself successful or unsuccessful in the eyes of others. Although society uses certain materialistic and monetary yardstick, to be considered successful you must be seen to act and behave successful."

"Ron, are you proposing that we should constantly talk about our successes?"

"No, on the contrary, Dan. If I have to constantly talk about my success, then I am not really successful. I do it to disguise my failures and to convince myself that I am successful. Such people are bitter with themselves, but it manifests in their pompous attitude towards others, whom they try to undermine and ridicule."

"Truly successful people rarely talk about their successes. They are humble and never boast of their success. They do not have to – they exude it."

"Thanks, Ron. I am wondering how I can determine what is success for me?" asked Dan.

"Good question. To answer this, we will first need to grasp an important concept."

"What we can control is our actions; although these actions influence it, the outcome or result is not in our hands as several external factors affect it."

"Mostly, we set results or outcome as our success measures; trying to achieve what is unpredictable and not in our direct control causes anxiety and frustrations. It distracts us from doing what is in our control — performing our actions and responsibilities with excellence."

Dan's face lit up and he spoke excitedly, "Ron this is so true. Thinking about my delayed promotion has been very distracting. It has not only caused frustration but has also affected my behavior and actions. The past few weeks have been so satisfying not only because of new learnings but also because promotion has not even been a thought; as if it is now irrelevant."

"Excellent! Your success measure has changed, Dan! Success is no longer the outcome of promotion but the actions of seek, soak, sift and share to convert new knowledge to learnings and putting those learnings to practice. It is satisfying because you are now focused on what is in your control."

"Yes, Ron. It is probably the most satisfying phase of my career."

"Can others feel your success in the past few weeks?" Ron asked with a smile.

"I do not know if they feel my success, but they see me more relaxed, more composed, more thoughtful, more understanding, more engaged, more smiling and at peace with myself." He hesitated shortly and continued, "I guess those are the telltale signs of success – probably they do feel my success."

"Until a few weeks back, success for you was promotion to director. As it was not happening, you were stressed, disappointed, distracted, and unable to focus on the only path that could take you there – performance. And in the process, you were moving further away from your perceived success -- promotion," Ron said.

"Over the past few weeks, your success criteria have changed to actions that are in your control. So, you have now started to experience successes."

"My personal example may probably help you understand it better. Do you think I would have made VP in such a short time if my success measure was to become VP?" asked Ron.

"I don't know, Ron."

"No. It would not have been possible. First, the outcome of becoming VP is not in my control. Second, I would not know what to do to become a VP. There are no defined actions. The inaction would have made me anxious and bitter, putting roadblocks in my progress."

"Instead, my success measure has always been to perform each of my assigned responsibilities and tasks to the best of my ability. Regular small wins and successes keep me inspired and motivated. I have never worried about the outcome – how my performance will be evaluated is my boss' problem; not mine. I have a conviction though, that if I perform my responsibilities to the best of my ability and with excellence, the outcome is inevitable. And I have been proven right; promotions have continued to come my way. Even today, I am least concerned about my next promotion. My focus is excellence in everything I do. That is all I can do; that is the only thing in my control!"

Dan was listening with rapt attention, mesmerized at this significant insight. The truth was staring at him somewhat mockingly – he was thinking how his continued anxiousness about his promotion had made him bitter, negatively impacting his work as well as his personal life.

His voice was frail when he spoke. "Ron, I wish someone had explained this to me several years back."

"Someone did, Dan. You may not recall but you and I had some conversations about this when you were my boss. You were probably not in learning mode then, I guess." He laughed.

Dan did not know where to look.

"We have covered quite a lot of ground already but have still not answered our original question. What do you think is your need for promotion, Dan?"

The question baffled Dan. He thought it was already answered; probably not. He was distraught briefly but gathered himself quickly. "Ron. It now appears I only had wants. Even success was a want."

"Is there a need that drives the want to be successful, Dan?"

"My successes in the past few weeks have made me happy. Could that have been the need?"

"Bingo! Thanks for your patience as I kept belaboring this

point. You have finally hit the nail on the head. Happiness it is. And this is the biggest travesty; although everything we do is in quest of happiness, we make it the source of our unhappiness," Ron said.

"The issue is that we search for happiness outside through external things – money, position, power, materialistic belongings – and it alludes us because happiness is intrinsic. External things bring momentary pleasures not happiness."

"Let me give you an analogy through an old fable," Ron continued. "The males of a particular Himalayan deer species have a unique gland that emanate musk fragrance. Not realizing that the source of the musk fragrance is within, the deer are constantly running across the forest in its search, instead of enjoying the fragrance. And in the process, they expose themselves and get hunted by musk poachers."

"Happiness is no different. We search for it everywhere and in everything, except within, and discover unhappiness. We constantly chase the mirage and not look at the oasis inside!"

"Your need was to be happy by becoming a director. But what did it do to you?"

Dan's voice was almost inaudible, "It brought a lot of anxiety and unhappiness."

"Do not feel bad. We all do this," Ron said.

"We talked about this earlier, but it is so important that I must repeat it. Only our action is in our control, not its outcome or result. Desired results or outcome are bound to come if we focus all our energies to perform our action – each duty and responsibility – to the best of our ability. Fretting over the outcome or results, which are not in our control, only causes stress, anxiousness, and unhappiness."

"Does this mean that we should not set any objective or goal,

Ron?"

"No. Define your purpose. Why are you working? Making money is an important reason but money can be made in 'x' number of ways. Money is not the only reason why you are here. There must be a higher purpose."

"Ron, it is quite ambiguous. It will probably become clearer if you do not mind describing your purpose?"

"I am glad you asked," Ron said. "I work because I am the only one who can make a unique difference using my unique skills. Nobody else can."

"That is a power statement. But isn't it too generic?"

"Yes, it is simple. Just think about it. How can Dan impact The Global Company?" He paused, looked straight into Dan's eyes, and continued, "By optimally utilizing his unique skills to make a unique difference that only Dan can."

"You don't compete against anyone but yourself; it is up to you to either keep enhancing your skills to continuously better your impact or not. It is also up to you to channel all your energy and effort on your actions, duties, and responsibilities or on worrying about other things like promotion, that are not in your control."

Dan was looking at Ron wide-eyed. When he spoke, his excited response was highly animated, "Ron, remember when I told you about the Indian concept of *guru*. On graduation, the *guru* reveals his final wisdom to each of the students, called *guru-mantra* – the secret to success and happiness; *mantra* is a hymn that the student is expected to invoke repeatedly. You have just revealed to me my *guru-mantra*."

"I researched the concept of guru after our discussion that day. I like it very much. Thank you for introducing it to me. I am aware of the *guru-mantra*. I did not realize that I was giving you one, though it is true that I believe you have now graduated." He said laughing.

"There is nothing more I can share. Although we have talked about it, let me now formally ask you if your questions and doubts, that brought you to me, have been satisfactorily answered?"

"Ron, you have given me far more than what I came for and was expecting. You have shown me the path. Now it is up to me. The past few weeks have been transformational for both my work and personal life. When I walked in here for the first time eight weeks back, little did I know that it was the best decision of my life. Your mindful attitude has given me a gift that I will cherish throughout," Dan said.

"You may want to know that the knowledge you imparted to me is benefiting many more beyond me. I am disseminating my learnings not only to my people but also to my friends. I have been able to retrieve not only mine but another marriage from the stage of apathy."

"That is outstanding," Ron said. "I am delighted to learn that it has benefitted you and that you are spreading the knowledge. Teaching or sharing, as we discussed, is the best way to learn."

"Dan you may be aware of the other ritual of the Indian *guru* tradition. The disciple gives '*guru-dakshna*', an offering to the guru, as a tribute to the wisdom received. Are you ready for your '*guru-dakshna*'?"

Shock would be an understatement to describe Dan's expressions. All he could manage to say, "Yes. Anything."

"Excellent." said Ron and paused for impact. "I need your commitment to pursue the learnings of the past few weeks unflinchingly and relentlessly. I want you to commit that irrespective of your promotion outcome you will not quit The

Global Company and spread this knowledge to as many people as you can."

"Color returned to Dan's face. "Ron, you have my commitment." He said with the bow of his head in reverence.

"Thanks." Ron smiled too, "I request that you convert this knowledge into a presentation. I want us to introduce it as a training module for all department managers in mastery function. I will talk to Bob Soros about making it mandatory training prior to section manager promotion. I will also discuss with global HR if they would like to introduce it companywide."

"It is a great idea, Ron. I would love to do it. What would you like to call this training?"

"Probably '**Success is a Choice.**' What do you think?"

Dan thought for a while, "I like it a lot. It summarizes my learnings of the past eight weeks succinctly so that anyone can choose to be successful."

"Before we close, Dan, I want to ask you one last question. Although we implied it, we did not discuss it specifically. But it is particularly important that we understand this."

"What is the relationship between success and happiness?"

Dan decided to practice ThERe as he wanted to bring the essence of all his learnings into this final answer to respect the honor of his 'graduation.' He was quiet, thinking, as Ron waited without any sign of impatience.

"Happiness is intrinsic and intangible. We can choose to either keep it locked in or set it free. Once out, it becomes tangible and obvious in our attitude, actions, behaviors, laughter, and smiles. It is infectious."

"Success is tangible and provides momentary pleasure and joy. It does not necessarily lead to happiness. Successful people are not necessarily happy, but happy people always believe in their success!"

"Wow! You have summed it up so beautifully Dan. With this we conclude our sessions."

"Finally, I want to complement you on your initiative and courage to seek help and come to me. Both critical behaviors of entrepreneurship skill of bold leadership. I wish you great success and happiness."

"We will keep meeting in the office for work and must also meet outside. As Nancy is much better now, let's plan an evening. I will have her call Betsy and set it up."

"I cannot thank you enough, Ron. Betsy and I look forward to meeting Nancy. Thank you."

They hugged and shook hands warmly.

Dan walked out of Ron's office with a smile on his face and a spring in his feet, ready to seize the world of happiness and success.

EPILOGUE

Five years have passed since Dan's new journey began in June 2011. A lot has changed, yet nothing has changed.

The Global Company has continued to grow at its customary pace; operations have started in a few more countries and a few more billion-dollar brands have been created. A new mandatory training, **Success Is a Choice** has been introduced for all newly promoted section managers. All current section managers, associate directors and directors have also been trained. The company has renewed its performance evaluation system to include potential and contribution as key assessment areas and has refocused it on improving potential skills and boosting strengths versus correcting weaknesses.

Amy Brown has never regretted her decision to stay back in The Global Company. Her project NG— to bring restaurant-like-flexibility in supply chains— has been expanded companywide. She became associate director two years ago.

Tom Adams could not make associate director despite Dan's significant efforts. Dan was deeply disappointed but realized that Tom was unable to share and practice what he was being taught. He left The Global Company four years back and joined a smaller corporation as director, a role almost equivalent to section manager in The Global Company. The news is that he is again in the job market because of stagnation.

Anne and Karan finally decided to start a family and are now proud parents of a lovely four-year-old girl and a cute one-year-old boy. They moved to India and have started a school to teach mindfulness to young children.

Johnathan graduated with a major in engineering; computer and information sciences and support services. He was hired by The Global Company through campus recruitment two years ago. He too is working in the mastery function but in a Pittsburgh factory. He owns and drives a Tesla Roadster.

Betsy and Dan have almost reached the expectation-free relationship, except when Dan gets delayed in the office. They completed their first expectations swap five years ago and renew it each year. The past five years have brought them much closer and made them happier than ever before. They visit Johnathan once a month and travel to different parts of the world every year. They spent four weeks with Anne and Karan in India last year.

Betsy is busier with her social work. She now leads her district and a team of fifty plus volunteers. Despite the expanded responsibilities and additional work, she feels far more relaxed and energetic.

Dan became director four-years-ago and was promoted again last year to vice president. He has occupied Ron's old office, with Linda Fernandes as his executive assistant. After instituting **Success Is a Choice** training in the mastery function, he is now companywide 'expert' for this training. He is mentoring Amy Brown and two other associate directors.

Ron Falcon became president of mastery function last year, reporting to the CEO. He now holds The Global Company record for fastest move to president. Several older VPs look at his meteoric rise with skepticism and wonder about the 'unfair' talent development system at The Global Company.

Somethings never change!

Dan's Learnings

I CREATE my HAPPINESS. Nothing external can!

I DEFINE my SUCCESS. Others only see what I show them!

I MAKE a UNIQUE DIFFERENCE through my unique skills. Nobody else can!

I PERFORM my RESPONSIBILITIES to the best of my ability. Result is only an outcome!

VALUE people and EMPOWER them to Peak Performance.

FEEL & THINK first. ASK to learn, LISTEN to understand. See and Show NONVERBALS effectively.

Clarify the INTENT before every conversation to prevent misinterpretation & misunderstanding.

Forego CONTROL to build & strengthen Relationships.

SELFLESSLY Care for people to INFLUENCE and gain COMMITMENT.

Use CONFLICTS as opportunity to ENGAGE.

SHARE new knowledge to create replicable LEARNING.

Define, Understand, Align, and Meet the NEEDS of every RELATIONSHIP.

Evaluate individual PERFORMANCE based on both, CONTRIBUTION & POTENTIAL.